RECYCLED ELEGANCE

Create a First-Class Lifestyle
Buying and Selling
Second-Hand Treasures

Aryana Delain

© 2016 Aryana Delain. All rights reserved. No part of this book may be reproduced without written permission from the author.

INTRODUCTION

The two large curio cabinets in the dining room were filled with dolls. There was an enormous dollhouse in the middle of the dining table. It was furnished with miniature Victorian furniture, fully functioning miniature lamps and even wallpaper. Who knew you can buy wallpaper for your dollhouse?

There were dolls on all the chairs and the walls were covered with deep frames, displaying doll rooms. Each one was furnished and had working electrical fixtures. In the years that I have been in the buying and selling business, I've seen lots of peculiar and amusing things, so this was not that unusual. *"Still, this is a unique way to use a dining room."* I thought.

As I looked around the room wondering where one would serve dinner to family and guests, since this was clearly the domain of the dolls, I heard myself asking *"How much do you want for all these?"* We had been discussing the contents of the two curio cabinets. My seller responded without hesitation *"Five hundred dollars"*.

The next morning I was eager to find out what my newly acquired doll collection was worth and "went to work" on it. By the following evening I was sitting on the floor of my spare bedroom watching a potential buyer inspect the dolls with a flashlight and the proverbial fine-tooth-comb. She worked silently and was taking a long time. This was beginning to feel like serious business…could my $500 investment turn into a few thousand dollars?

Moments like these are what make this business so much fun...the excitement and the anticipation! It was a good thing I was sitting down, because you could have knocked me over with a feather when she said "I have to mortgage my house to do it, but I'm prepared to pay you **$65,000** for the collection!"

CONTENTS

CHAPTER 1, THE BEST BUSINESS IN THE WORLD 1

CHAPTER 2, "PENNIES ON THE DOLLAR" THINKING 8

CHAPTER 3, PROFITS, PROFITS AND MORE PROFITS! 20

CHAPTER 4, WHERE ARE THE TREASURES? 28

CHAPTER 5, HOW TO SHOP AT
GARAGE/ESTATE/MOVING SALES..46

CHAPTER 6, THE FINE ART OF BARGAINING 72

CHAPTER 7, SELLING YOUR TREASURES
FOR MEGA PROFITS 98

CHAPTER 8, YOU TOO CAN MAKE $4,657
AT YOUR GARAGE SALE 116

CHAPTER 9, PENNIES ON THE DOLLAR DECORATING 137

CHAPTER 10, CHRISTMAS EVERY DAY.................................156

CHAPTER 11, WHAT NOT TO DO..164

CHAPTER 12, FOCUS AND DISCIPLINE
EQUALS WEALTH 179

CHAPTER 1

THE BEST BUSINESS IN THE WORLD

Yes, you read it right. I bought the dolls for $500 and sold them for $65,000! The hardest part was keeping a business-like demeanor and not jumping up and down while counting the cash!

I have been fortunate to live the adventurous life of a treasure hunter….someone who buys valuable things for pennies on the dollar and resells them for extraordinary profits. The dolls were just one of many exciting moments along the way.

This book is the culmination of my expertise, the tricks and priceless knowledge from this amazing entrepreneurial business that I am so grateful to have found at a young age. It has afforded me a first class, fun and exciting lifestyle, while being free of a conventional J-O-B. My time is my own, and in my opinion, that is the greatest freedom of all. I don't have to put up with a demanding boss or unpleasant co-workers and most glorious of all, if I don't feel like going to work…I simply don't. I don't wake up to an alarm clock jolting me out of bed and I don't sit in traffic. I never think of the day when I get to retire, because I love what I do and I don't consider it 'work'. This is living life on your own terms and it's not only fun, it's also exciting and very lucrative. If you were ordering the perfect "job", wouldn't those be the things on your list?

THE BEST BUSINESS IN THE WORLD

Through the years, many people have asked me to teach them to do what I do, to share with them the secrets of this exciting money making business. Until recently, I never considered doing such a thing. After all, why would I teach other people to compete with me? I will explain what led me to write this book, and why I am willing to give away the secrets to a business that for more than 30 years has been a most amazing income stream.

I came to California in the mid-nineties to take a seminar on acquiring real estate and personal property through probate. It was a $6,000 workshop teaching the secrets of how the probate system works and the fantastic deals that were available to anyone willing to look for them. The majority of the attendees were wealthy real estate investors.

After moving to California, I got involved with the company and spent time traveling all over the country where the workshops were held. There was a heavy emphasis for the students on real estate, and I came to realize that while lots of people knew about buying real estate, they didn't have much knowledge about buying personal property. Because this was exactly my area of expertise, one day I found myself teaching the class. It was fun to watch a group of wealthy (mostly men) investors look at me doubtfully, wondering what this woman in the hot-pink suit could possibly teach them about personal property. What could I have to say about "stuff" that would be of interest to them?

Most people don't have a clue about the profit potential of buying and selling personal property, or *treasures*, as I call them. The best part was watching everyone's face change from mild curiosity to interest and then to enthusiasm and finally to excitement! By explaining the endlessly exciting world of turning 'stuff' into cash, I had converted a room full of hard-core real estate investors! In the course of sharing my passion, I discovered a new passion....teaching. It took a few years until I actually got around to writing this book but right now is the perfect time to learn this business because it will serve you well for the rest of your life.

At this time, global as well as individual economies are taking quite a roller-coaster ride and now more than ever, we need a new way of doing the old things. The information in this book could change your life in a very significant way. This is not a get-rich-quick scheme, but like the woman who recently bought a painting for $10 and sold it for $2 million at auction, the possibility for instant riches is very real.

While you keep an eye out for that one treasure that would buy you the villa in Italy or a carefree life on a yacht in the Mediterranean, you will live interesting and exciting days and a life filled with adventure and fun. What more could you possibly ask for? Oh yes, let's not forget....lots of money!

When it comes to the endless list of things that people desire, you can be sure that countless others have already purchased everything on that list and *their* main desire now is to get rid of it. While the emphasis for you is on a fabulous income, I want to be sure to point out that there are numerous other benefits as well. I want to show you how to acquire the things on *your* desire list for a fraction of their original cost. It's almost like creating financial freedom through spending. Imagine furnishing your home with the most unique and beautiful décor from all over the world...for pennies on the dollar, without ever touching your credit card.

In fact, the title of this book should be...."*PENNIES ON THE DOLLAR*" because whatever you buy, that is the price you will pay. When you see the endless stream of beautiful, expensive things that can be yours for ridiculously low prices, you'll begin to move away from buying retail. I will teach you where to look, but the *mind-shift* is up to you.

A few years ago when I was remodeling my house, I bought a brand new $3,000 dollar name-brand double paned French door for $300. The people who sold it were also remodeling their home and months earlier bought several doors and apparently one too many.

Once your home is all finished, what are you going to do with a large door taking up space in your garage? Simple...you want to be free of it. At that point people are not looking to recover the money they originally spent...that's history. They just want closure and they don't want to look at it another day. The seller was as happy and grateful to me for taking it off his hands, as I was to be buying it...for 10 cents on the dollar!

A few months ago I saw an interview on TV with a man who found an interesting brooch in a junk store. He paid $14 for it and the reason for the interview was that his $14 brooch turned out to be worth over $600,000. While it was a gorgeous piece, it was the extremely rare type of pearl in the center setting that made it so valuable. He had no idea that the pearl had such value; he only bought it because he recognized excellent workmanship and that made him think it was gold and thought it likely that the other stones were diamonds.

This story is so simple and typical of the possibilities that exist in this business. The person buying the brooch saw something that was obviously unique and beautiful and risked fourteen whole dollars. It didn't take a genius or a degree to do this; only someone who was out having fun looking for treasures....seek and you shall find!

A few months ago I bought 2 huge red flower pots that someone paid a whopping $800 for in a retail store. They were happy to have me take the heavy things off their hands for...would you believe $40? This was at a garage sale, and it was almost noon! These pots were gorgeous...was everybody sleeping? Had a savvy shopper (which is what you will be) come along, they would have snapped them up and turned their $40 into at least $300. This book will show you exactly how it's done.

I came home with a brand new St. John Knit jacket that retails for $1,200 and I bought it for an unbelievable $30! I found another designer evening gown with the $900 tag still on it, for an unbelievable $5. I discovered my Vita-Mix blender that retails for $599, under a table at a garage sale, in an unopened box for $35. Just a few weeks ago I bought two gold rings for $5 each. One even had diamonds in it! The other one was heavy rose gold with beautiful workmanship and a heart-shaped amethyst stone.

I mention elsewhere that one of my friends found two little oil paintings for $8 each which sold for $2,000 each at an auction. She bought them because she liked the frames and had no idea they were valuable. With just a little bit of additional work and research she made a lot more money!

Many years ago I found six Vargas prints (the artist whose voluptuous female drawings were featured in Playboy magazine) for $1 each and sold them for $100 each. Six dollars turned into $600 overnight...where else can you do that? One of my favorites was the shoe box full of collectible miniatures that I bought for $20 and sold for $7800 the next day!!

It is my desire is to show people that with a small shift in their thinking they will begin to notice the opportunities all around them. Don't worry; retail shopping won't come to a screeching halt. We don't want that to happen, everyone needs to make a living and retailers are a necessary part of our economic structure.

We are simply looking for the **bargains that already exist** and diverting some of the treasures and some of the profits our way. The wonderful news is that treasures are everywhere, all around you. When I started in this business, I did it on my own. Nobody taught me anything. The truth is that I didn't even realize I was in a business. While my family was buying cute things for themselves at garage sales, I started to think about re-selling some of the cute things I had accumulated.

Over the years I've been told many times that I have excellent taste and I often wondered if it's something I was born with, or if it's something anyone can learn. I was born in a small town in a Europe and at the time my country was under communist regime.

We didn't have indoor plumbing or many of the other luxuries that in America were considered basic necessities and I wouldn't have known Louis Vuitton from Louis the butcher. I was certainly not born into a world of fine wines, Baccarat crystal or Chanel No.5. In fact, we didn't even have electricity until I was 6 years old!

Yet, here I am years later, able to distinguish something of value without even touching it. Because of my expertise I've been flown in private planes on more than one occasion to evaluate treasures. How is this possible? More importantly can anyone do it? Yes, absolutely anyone can do it!

I believe that **desire** is the fundamental key to mastering anything. I'm certain that once you get a taste for the *treasure business* and the affluent lifestyle you can create for pennies on the dollar, you will fall in love with it and your ability to recognize things of value will get stronger and soon become second nature.

This isn't just a business; it's a way of life. Anyone can master the contents of this book and by doing so, open doors to a life-time of exciting opportunities. You now hold the map to a fun-filled path to riches along with the key to the treasure chest. It's time to make YOUR dreams come true!

CHAPTER 2

"PENNIES ON THE DOLLAR" THINKING

A few years ago I got a call from an acquaintance who had just bought an amazing vacuum cleaner guaranteed to stop allergies. She was excited and asked if I would be willing to let someone come over and show me the benefits of this new-age wonder vacuum.

I was caught off guard and agreed to a demonstration in my home. As I watched the demo and realized the health benefits and all around brilliant concept of the vacuum, I got caught up in the moment and agreed to buy it. I was doing something I rarely do: impulse buying in the retail market.

I ended up paying a ridiculous $1,800 for that vacuum cleaner! After it was too late to change my mind, I saw that I could have bought the same exact thing on eBay for under $500! Ouch! I still have the vacuum and I still love it, but I threw away $1,300 for absolutely no reason. Sadly, too many people do this on a regular basis.

I know that some folks wouldn't dream of buying anything second-hand, if their life depended on it, but if you ask them why, they're at a loss to come up with any valid reasons. Retailers have done a very thorough job convincing us that unless something comes directly from them, it's not desirable.

We simply get used to doing something without ever questioning the logic behind our actions.

In 2011, Nike footwear had an unbelievable $2.4 billion dollar advertising budget. Last year there were at least 38 companies that spent over one billion dollars on advertising. The business world is very competitive with too many retailers out there fighting over your money. They have extremely well-formulated and very compelling campaigns, but where does all that leave you?

Advertising is the trap that's designed to appeal to our ego. Sometimes our mind succeeds in talking us out of being logical and we just want to whip out that credit card and go crazy. If our ego stands in the way of a better life, it's helpful to re-examine some of our old programmed beliefs.

Did I say a better life? How can someone have a better life by buying used things? In fact some might be inclined to say that buying second hand items is a step backwards and a decline in lifestyle. But they couldn't be more wrong!

Because our actions are based on our thoughts I feel it's important to address the psychological aspect of what I teach. In order for someone to apply it, it has to make sense and nothing gets people's attention more than making sense about their money.

Consider the fact that there is one reason most people have a job...that reason is **money**. Also consider the fact that it's what that money can buy that we are actually wanting, not the pieces of paper.

"PENNIES ON THE DOLLAR" THINKING

After paying for the basic necessities, we want money so we can buy the things that make us *feel good*.

We want a nice home filled with things that are an expression of our own personal taste and we want personal possessions that we think will enhance our lives. The finer things in life are the details; never the necessities….they are simply pleasing to our senses. Whether it's a luxury car or a motorcycle, theater tickets or snowboarding, our lifestyle, the way we spend money after our food-and-shelter needs are met is what's important to us as individuals. It is the only reason we go looking for this thing called a JOB in the first place.

I was helping a friend with an estate sale recently and while pricing a vase I was thinking about how we, as a society, spend our money. The vase was one of those new décor items that have flooded the American market, made in China with no value other than the fact that it fills up space. The $20 price tag was still on the bottom and since a decorative vase really doesn't get used, you could say it was new.

If you take an average salary of let's say $10 dollars per hour someone would have to work two hours to buy that meaningless little vase. Adding sales tax to the purchase price and deducting income tax from the salary, now we're closer to two and a half hours. And let's not forget that some people earn less than $10 per hour.

Imagine that you're at the end of a long day at work, looking forward to getting home to your family or simply to relax and unwind from the endless hassles of another day on the job. Just as you're ready to walk out, your boss stops you and shows you this $20 vase and tells you that if you stay late and work two more hours you can have it. What would you say? In that context any sane person would be offended to be taken for a fool...that you would trade two of your most valuable commodities, your time and energy, for something so worthless.

Yet this is exactly how most of us squander our money and our time. We have completely restructured China's economy by doing just that. While we would say *no* in the above scenario, we say *yes* when we go shopping in retail stores. The mind-boggling amount of American dollars that have turned a poor communist country into an economic powerhouse is a sad testimony to how disconnected we are from the way we spend our hard earned dollars. Giant corporations invest billions of dollars to manipulate our spending habits. They tell us what to eat, what to wear, what to read, what to drive and what to think.

Saddest of all is that when it falls apart, as all corrupt, self- perpetuating entities eventually do, the ones who suffer the fallout are the people who never even knew they were being used and manipulated. When our economic train recently derailed the ones who were hit the hardest were the average families. Suddenly going from the *American Dream* to "survival mode" has become a harsh and devastating reality for too many Americans.

Life has been arranged for us in a way that we don't spend money anymore...we just reach for a card. We have become disconnected from the fact that we have to work a certain number of hours for everything we buy. The credit card has to be paid back and if you add the ridiculous interest rates that credit card

"PENNIES ON THE DOLLAR" THINKING

companies charge, that $20 vase would now cost you more than three hours of your precious time.

Time is our greatest commodity and if we squander it on trinkets we soon have nothing to show for it except the mounting credit card debts. For many people it's become a vicious cycle that keeps them living on a treadmill.

As I was wondering what to price the vase it occurred to me that even if I tag it $5 which would be 75% off the retail cost, it would still be overpriced and someone would still have to work at least a half hour to buy it.

Now that we looked at the bad news, let's look at some good news. The good news is that if you are willing to give up the idea that you have to buy things new in a retail store, you will become a brilliant shopper and you can fill your home with beautiful things while holding on to a lot more of your money.

As for the idea of only wanting things that are new; here is a concept to consider… everything you buy from someone else will be new…**new to you,** and that's all that matters.

If you take a moment and reflect on your past purchases, do you remember how long the excitement of buying something new lasted? Not very long…you use it, put it on the shelf or hang it in the closet and life goes on. Even your most exciting purchase will have lost its luster long before you finish paying for it on your credit card.

It simply doesn't make sense to buy over-priced things in retail stores. Shopping at garage/estate/

moving sales and browsing the classifieds can become an exciting way of life. With online auctions from all over the world and in every category, there is even less reason to buy retail.

I don't rush out in December to buy Christmas cards because I already have plenty of high-quality, expensive cards that I found during the summer for pennies. I also have a box with cards for every occasion all organized and never have to rush last minute.

You only have to set this system up once and it will save you hours of aggravation and ultimately hundreds of dollars. Life is too busy to allow minor details to disrupt your peace of mind. Same with wrapping paper and gift bags; I have plenty on hand. This is efficient time management and puts an end to the very costly habit of last minute chasing.

I remember one occasion running around with a friend doing last minute shopping. We were going to a birthday party and while she had bought a gift the day before, for $40, she didn't have paper at home to wrap it, so we drove to the nearest drugstore. By the time she bought a card, wrapping paper and tape, along with a bow and a gift bag, all she got back from her $20 was change! Wow! Talk about throwing $20 right into the trash!

She signed the card and wrapped the box in the car while I drove. She was frazzled to say the least and it took her a half hour and a cocktail to calm down. What a waste of money and energy! Too many people live this way, but it's truly unnecessary.

"PENNIES ON THE DOLLAR" THINKING

As I also mention in another chapter, I have a cabinet where I keep gifts ready to go at a moment's notice. They are interesting and unique pieces in various price ranges and they all came from garage/estate/moving sales. I have a selection of beautiful costume jewelry, men's silk ties, perfumes, trinkets and décor items and I am sure to find the perfect gift for anyone and everyone among my own inventory.

When I need a gift for someone, I shop in my own cabinet and choose from things that I already selected because of their beauty or one-of-kind appeal. What I DO NOT do, is waste my valuable time at the mall looking through things that are overpriced and then talk myself into buying something because I'm running out of time. While my friend spent sixty stressful dollars for the party, I spent five relaxed happy dollars.

I hope you're getting excited about using your time and your money in a better way. My gifts always stand out and often I just like to give them for no reason at all. I love knowing that for a few dollars I can add a little bit of joy to someone's life. This is so much fun! I ran into someone just the other day and she was wearing a pin I had given her. She said she gets compliments on it constantly and loves it. I paid exactly one dollar for that pin and love the fact that it's still making someone's day a bit brighter.

I also remember what my friends like and when I see something they would like, I buy it for them. When one of my friends was looking for a nightstand I found a very attractive one in brand new condition for only $15!

The nightstand was an excellent deal, especially when that same $15 wouldn't even buy the previously mentioned vase in a retail store. When you see how much fun it is to shop like this and the unbelievable prices you find, you will get very excited about living your life this way.

The same place I bought the nightstand I spotted an old stained glass window décor which I bought for only $5. I took it to a local consignment store and they sold it for $225!

I was not the first person at that garage sale. In fact, it was mid- morning by the time I got there and I was not even among the first 25 shoppers. The deals were still there because the people who had been there before me were not using *pennies on the dollar* thinking.

The average person goes to garage sales only to browse and not with an entrepreneurial mind-set to buy and re-sell things for a profit.

At this particular garage sale the items were not priced and people sometimes hesitate to ask prices unless they have a definite level of interest. There seems to be some silly notion not to over-burden the sellers with questions. So there sat this beautiful antique stained glass piece leaning against a post for the absurd asking price of $5. Some people didn't see it and others simply didn't see the opportunity.

The nightstand was a steal and would have sold in a consignment store for at least $150. The nightstand and stained glass cost me a total of $20. Had I taken both to a consignment store, they would have sold for $375, and half of that would have gone

"PENNIES ON THE DOLLAR" THINKING

to me. That's a profit of $167.50 from one little garage sale where I spent less than fifteen minutes.

It's exciting and rewarding to get checks in the mail from consignment stores after you have just about forgotten about the item. I once bought a vintage Chanel dress for $20 and was quite surprised to receive a check for $1,100 as my share of the sale from a high-end consignment boutique!

Hopefully by the time you finish this book, you will be one of the few who asks prices and checks out everything at every garage sale. You will be an alert and savvy shopper. You will be mastering the art of **pennies on the dollar** thinking when you buy and **dollars on the pennies** when you sell. It all adds up and before you know it, your lifestyle will be wealthier and definitely more peaceful.

It is my sincere desire to inspire you to think *outside the box* while teaching you skills that empower you to know that you can survive and even thrive without a job. Your security is in your own hands not in a company that may or may not be around tomorrow. For a better lifestyle and peace of mind, it's imperative to examine our spending habits and the best way to start is by remembering how many hours we have to work for every single thing we buy.

I wrote this book to show people that it's completely unnecessary to spend so much of their hard-earned dollars on everyday things. You will be amazed how good you feel when you are in control of your spending and even more amazed that you can have better quality things than ever before and spend far less than ever before.

Certain people have not been singled out as better, or more deserving than others. That's just ridiculous, it's a lie that was sold to us and following someone else's belief in lack and limitation is foolish.

If you want a better and richer life, you should have it. There is absolutely no reason to deny yourself the things that bring you joy and with a little planning you can have them easily in a short amount of time.

Everything is outlined for you in this book and once you change your thoughts and subsequently your habits, you will never look back. Every single person who has adopted this way of life has been immensely happier and wealthier because if it.

You will be thrilled to buy things for pennies on the dollar for yourself and your family and even more thrilled by creating large amounts of cash from your *pennies on the dollar* purchases.

I read somewhere that the average American household would benefit immensely from just a few hundred dollars a month extra income. Fortunately, you no longer need to wait for someone to give you a pay-raise. You can give it to yourself and if you apply what you learn in this book, you soon will be making a lot more money than you ever expected.

You will also be empowering yourself to become an entrepreneur and building confidence that you can take care of yourself and your family without relying on your job or the government. By becoming self-reliant, you can set yourself free and get off the treadmill.

"PENNIES ON THE DOLLAR" THINKING

When you broaden your horizons and think outside the box (outside the job) you will be amazed how many other opportunities come your way. Our thoughts create our reality and having confidence in ourselves is the greatest asset we can cultivate. That confidence will give you courage, and it will move you forward toward bigger deals and a higher income bracket.

I found my first house while looking at furniture and paid less than half of market value. Some people may find it difficult to believe, but I bought several pieces of real estate and never, ever paid more than 50 cents on the dollar.

It's been exhilarating for me to live life on my own terms, not having to rely on someone else for the money or the benefits. I am free to travel and see the world and come and go as I please, to set my own schedule…all because I learned this fantastic business a long time ago.

If you choose to keep your job it should be because you enjoy it and because you are treated like a valued team member. You're there because you choose to be, **not** because you have to be. In my opinion, that's freedom.

Freedom and the self-confidence in your ability to handle your own life will make you a much happier person. Happy people have more energy and a sense of well-being. People who feel in control of their life take better care of themselves and they live fully. They manage their time better and are never too busy for their children, their loved ones and everything else that is important in life.

RECYCLED ELEGANCE

    Stressed out, frazzled people living on junk food, coffee and adrenaline and rushing through life tend to create a lot of havoc. They attract accidents and one crisis after another and don't realize until it's too late that they forgot to live.

CHAPTER 3

PROFITS, PROFITS AND MORE PROFITS!

The first question everyone asks is: Why would anyone sell valuables for pennies? Followed by: Why would someone sell such a valuable doll collection for $500? Why didn't **they** just sell it for $65,000? As difficult as all this may be to believe, it gets even crazier.

A couple of days after discovering that my newly acquired doll collection was the deal of the year, I received an interesting phone call from the seller. He wanted to be sure to let me know that I shouldn't sell the dolls too cheap because he had a $34,000 insurance policy on them! Even I was dumb-founded!

He also asked me to come back to look at other things that he wanted to get rid of. In subsequent visits I bought all the doll houses and the antique curio cabinets that had been used to store the dolls.

I also bought all the Lladro figurines and other porcelains, lots of other antiques, collectibles, and vintage items, a gorgeous antique amethyst lamp and lots of spectacular and valuable jewelry. These were among the things that he wanted to "get rid of".

What makes people do such crazy things? In all my years in this business I have had an ongoing fascination for how individuals handle their personal property. Human behavior is infinitely interesting and when it comes to people and their *stuff* sometimes it goes from interesting to downright bizarre. My friend "Sam" with the dolls was certainly one of these interesting characters.

To say that Sam was not a good housekeeper would be an understatement. His wife had passed away several years earlier and I suspect the last time he took a shower was while she was still alive. He had a condo in a beautiful, well-kept building and the association was sending him threatening letters because his unit had an unpleasant smell emanating from it and the neighbors were complaining. It did not occur to Sam that his little dog had to do *all* his bathroom duties outside...if he didn't feel like taking him out, he simply didn't. The last time the sheets on the bed were changed was probably the same year that he took his last shower.

On my first visit after I bought a few items in the living room I couldn't wait to get out of there and breathe some fresh air. I was already walking out the door when he asked if I wanted to buy some dolls. I asked where they were and he pointed down a long hallway to the dining room. I was in a hurry to get out and for a second I thought of saying no, but I couldn't leave without checking out what other treasures might be available. The hallway seemed to be a mile long because I was holding my breath along the way, but the dining room was extremely interesting.

I didn't know anything about dolls and I had never bought one before. I am constantly asked if I specialize in anything and I want to repeat that the only specialty I have and what I teach is: **making money**. Many people specialize in things that are of

PROFITS, PROFITS AND MORE PROFITS!

interest to them and I think they miss out on a lot of opportunities. I have personal preferences and things I personally collect, but why would I want to limit myself to just one area when it comes to good deals? Remember to think outside the box.

Going back to the dolls; I had no idea they were so valuable. There were two large cabinets full, so I figured that they had to be worth more than the price he was asking. The prices on the figurines I had just bought from him were very reasonable, so he had already established himself as a motivated seller with great prices. As it turned out three of the dolls were a hundred years old French bisque and those three were worth over $25,000!

I could have gone crazy thinking my future riches would be in the doll collecting arena and learn everything about dolls and specialize in dolls. I don't really like dolls and learning about something I am not passionate about would be tedious and too much like 'work'. I would have also destroyed my financial career because the truth is that I have not seen a noteworthy doll since. At least none that were worth more than a few hundred dollars.

Sam later told me that he had always hated all the "junk" his wife collected and he especially hated the dolls. He thought that because they were old they must be the source of the smell or as he put it the dolls were "holding the smell" and the condo board was getting nasty about it.

He didn't bother to call anyone else or get other offers. I was there and I was it. He never expressed the slightest regret about selling something so heavily insured for next to nothing. He was quite relieved to have them gone and as I said earlier, he asked me to come back several times and take other things off his hands.

Though Sam's housekeeping and grooming habits were sorely lacking and his manners were also quite rough, he was far from stupid. He read the papers daily and followed the stock market and had numerous investments.

The condo was in a great area and the contents were expensive and elegant and obviously chosen by a wife who had excellent taste. Collecting valuable dolls is not a hobby for people with money problems and I'm sure that Sam was more than comfortable financially. His motivation was to get rid of the smell and to get rid of the stuff that he hated. It's that simple.

Above all you have to let go of the idea that people use common sense and logic in their daily lives. If there is one great message in all the amazing deals that I have come across in my forty plus years; it would be to expect the unexpected.

Don't get in your own way by trying to figure out what could be wrong here because you personally would never do anything so dumb. Don't let the good deals pass you by while you linger in disbelief.

A few years ago, when I had a consignment business, I met a lady who wanted to consign a sofa and some very nice high-end furniture. They had remodeled their home and were in the process of finishing the family room. She was explaining to me that they paid $11,000 dollars just a few months

PROFITS, PROFITS AND MORE PROFITS!

earlier for the sofa but now they had to get rid it because it didn't match the color of the walls.

I couldn't resist asking the obvious question; why they didn't just repaint the walls instead of tossing a brand new $11,000 dollar sofa. She said they already did that 3 times and they finally liked the current shade of beige.

Were they serious...the perfect shade of beige? This was no cheap paint job either! They had a very expensive paint job redone 3 times by a very expensive painter and when she showed me the samples I could barely detect any difference!

The casualty of this insanity was the poor little sofa. Although it was custom ordered with expensive fabric and stunning pillows, they had grossly and ridiculously overpaid for the brand name. To compound the problem, the look and style of it was country with lots of blue and therefore limited appeal. I thought she might want to shoot the messenger when I said they would be lucky to get $500 for their $11,000 sofa but her only response was to ask how fast I could get it out of her house.

As is typical in these cases, they simply didn't care. They had already made up their mind to get rid of it. Emotionally they had let go of the little country couch and now this lady was looking to me to make it go away. I was the one she expected to solve her problem.

I solved it by taking it off her hands and putting it on consignment in my store. She got $800 for the $11,000 sofa and was grateful while I was downright disturbed that they were content to throw away $10,200 to keep their shade of beige wall color!

People do this kind of crazy stuff all the time because they simply don't care. Human nature is what it is and that's why there is no end to this wonderful business. People do what they do and someone will get the deal….it might as well be you.

Here's a funny story: I was looking at some items in a house once sitting across from a seriously busy woman who was trying to tell me between her phone calls and family running in and out that she wanted everything gone because she wanted to remodel that room. I gave her what I thought was a rather low price and she agreed immediately. I went out to the car to get my purse, so I could write her a check and by the time I came back, she had written *me* a check! That was a first! She had been asking for the price on how much to pay me for taking the stuff!

Before I could say something her phone rang again and I couldn't sit through another of her phone calls, but the next day I went back to clear up the misunderstanding and return her check. After she stopped laughing, she thanked me and accepted her check back. She would however, not accept any money from me, so I got everything in the room free, which added up to around $3,000 dollars in resale.

I never quite understood what she had been thinking, but on subsequent visits I bought jewelry from her, very inexpensively and a few great vintage evening dresses, some of which I still have. Guess who got the rest of the furniture as she kept remodeling the house? I cannot say it enough; this is a very rewarding, wonderful business!

PROFITS, PROFITS AND MORE PROFITS!

When you put rational thinking aside and understand that for most people it's not about the money, you'll stop doubting the good deals and allow them to flow. In this business **if it's too good to be true.....buy it!** That's the whole idea; we want all our deals to be too good to be true.

We all know the old saying that one man's trash is another man's treasure. I wish I had come up with that line, because it's absolutely true a million times a day across the country and across the globe. And we're talking about some very serious treasures!

One of my favorite stories is the woman who was selling 18k gold jewelry for 25 cents each piece. I mean stunning, beautiful jewelry with diamonds and other precious stones. She was asking 25 cents for the rings and 25 cents for the earrings. After I bought everything she had, I couldn't resist asking her why she would sell gold jewelry for twenty five cents, while the used toaster was priced at $5.

Her incredible explanation was that she thought all her gold was from Europe or Asia and it wasn't American gold...therefore according to her, it had to be worthless. Wow! You simply can't argue with that kind of logic! And I didn't want to argue...I was there for the deal, not to set her straight.

It is not my place to educate or enlighten sellers. We all live in the same world and have access to the same resources. In my early days I used to get more involved, but people don't listen and they end up resenting you for making them look stupid. So, I rarely say anything to anyone, with the possible exception of an older person, who may appear to need some help. And I'm referring only to things that

I'm not personally interested in buying. If I'm buying it, I never work against myself by telling someone they should charge me more. That's crazy!

Many years ago I was at a sale and a lady was kind enough to point out to the seller that the high-end designer handbag she was selling for $5.00 was worth a small fortune and she should ask a lot more for it. The seller thanked her politely, and after the woman left she put it back on the table, where I grabbed it for $5.00 I ended up with what indeed was an extremely valuable purse. Lesson learned.

Besides, while I hang around showing off how much I know and telling others what they should be doing, someone else is running off with my stuff at the next garage sale. Let's stay focused and keep moving!

CHAPTER 4

WHERE ARE THE TREASURES?

Another of the frequently asked questions I get is: "Where do you find all the goodies?" The big-picture answer is that where there are people, there are treasures. Your playing field is anywhere and everywhere. When I tell people what I do, they either know of somebody or they personally have things they want to sell.

If you listen to someone talk and you hear the words "*get rid of*" it's a good bet that you are talking to a motivated seller. People divorce themselves mentally and emotionally from things they want to "*get rid of*". When speaking of something we value, we tend to use the word "sell". Most people don't "*get rid of*" their house, or the Rolls-Royce or the Rolex watch.

Don't let this trip you up however, because the things that you would never put in the category of *get rid of* items, other people most certainly would. We all have a different value system and to the person who only buys expensive designer clothes and $1500 handbags, when it's time to let it go, it's time to *get rid of* it.

The best place to start looking for things is **garage sales**. Before you dismiss this idea as silly or useless let me say that I have been going to garage sales since I was a teenager and truly they can be the best resource for undervalued treasures. It seems too simple because people want elaborate tricks and complex systems, but don't let the simplicity fool you.

I give you many other methods in this book and the tricks and systems that I learned along the way, but it's best to start with the basics. The very fact that many people refuse to go to garage sales is the reason that **you** should be going. If you want to be successful, do the opposite of what the crowd is doing.

I got hooked on garage sales as a teenager in the seventies and I have found the most incredible deals along the way. I bought unbelievable amounts of jewelry, designer clothes, fabulous art, furniture and anything else one can imagine.

Not long ago I found a sweater decorated with pieces of fur and turquoise jewelry that looked very interesting. There was a pair of matching leggings that came with it and because it was starting to rain, I just grabbed it all thinking I would use the beautiful decorations on it for something else. When I got home, I saw that not only was it brand new, but it turned out to be a seriously expensive designer outfit. When I tried it on, I was thrilled to find that it's one of those unique one-of-a-kind ensembles that I go crazy over and I would have happily paid a couple of hundred dollars for it. Lucky for me, I didn't have to...all she wanted was one dollar.

My home is decorated with high-end furniture and some very expensive accent pieces, but more importantly all these unique and beautiful things that reflect my taste came from sales. The only furniture

WHERE ARE THE TREASURES?

stores I visit are consignment stores. The variety of beautiful pieces from different homes and different time periods is interesting and exciting. Buying overpriced junk made in China is not.

I mention elsewhere that recently I bought two exquisite 18k gold rings (one with diamonds) for $5 each. The best part is that these treasures are everywhere and with minimum effort anyone can find them.

The list goes on and on, all purchased from someone for pennies on the dollar. I have even bought piggy-banks containing money, because the owner just didn't care to open it and take the money out. Let's not forget the thousands of dollars I have found throughout the years that people left in purses and pockets.

Many times it turned out that I paid people with their own money. The money they negligently left in pockets or purses or wallets, or drawers. I once found three crisp one hundred dollar bills in the pocket of a coat and another five hundred dollars in various purses and pockets from someone who charged me $35 for everything. Another time I found $300 in a purse. Countless times, after spending all day, I ended up going home with more money than I stared with.

In case you are wondering; no, I didn't go back and give people the money. First of all when you go from sale to sale it's impossible to remember where you bought what item. Secondly, if someone doesn't care enough to do that for themselves, it's not up to me to go chasing after them. It's completely their responsibility. How much effort is required to open a purse or check a pocket? Much less than it would take me to run around trying to re-unite someone with the money they carelessly abandoned.

I was recently chatting with a friend who has a prominent clock shop in the area and he was telling me stories of people who had consigned very expensive items with him and then moved away never to be heard from again, or had left large deposits on expensive clocks and never came back.

When I had a store, I had many similar experiences. I once sold a very expensive antique desk for a couple who moved away with no forwarding address and never bothered to call about their money. People don't care; they are either too busy or too careless.

The American garage sale is an amazing institution. If I could go back and add up all the money I have made from garage sales most people would not believe it. It's a fun and easy method for finding deals. You can do it anywhere, any state across the nation! One day I would like to garage sale shop my way across the country. If you want to become a successful treasure-broker don't pooh-pooh garage sales and don't underestimate the opportunities for finding treasures.

For those of you, who still think that you couldn't possibly find anything valuable at a garage sale, I want to tell you about John, a friend's brother who bought a lamp at a garage sale some years ago for $30. The lamp he bought turned out to be a signed Tiffany piece that was subsequently appraised for $85,000. He found that lamp at a garage sale, at the end of the day and it was still sitting there because nobody wanted it.

Along with garage sales, we also have **moving sales.** This is pretty self-explanatory….people are moving and for one reason or another they are not taking everything with them. I consider garage and moving sales to be just about the same thing. It's a ***get rid of*** sale and remembering that one man's junk is another man's treasure, you want to be there when they are getting rid of the "junk".

Another type of sale that falls under this category is an **estate sale**. This is when someone passes away and their "estate" (personal belongings) is sold. Estate sales are often conducted by companies who do all the work for a percentage of the total profit. They are professionals and they research the values and price the items accordingly.

A professionally conducted estate sale is probably not going to be the place that sells gold rings for a quarter. The family hires these companies because they themselves don't know values and don't know the first thing about doing a sale.

It can take a couple of weeks to organize one of these and to research and tag everything. Having conducted many estate sales I can tell you from an organizers perspective, they are a lot of work. While you can find some very interesting things at estate sales, if the company did their job right, you won't be finding the deal of the century, or even the deal of the year. You are not supposed to; that's why they hired professionals.

You may find some outstanding items at nice prices and I would certainly not miss one, if I were you. An estate sale is also great for your continuing education. You can check out the prices and just observe what people are buying, as well as what they are not buying.

If you are serious about this business you might ask one of these companies for a job or even volunteer to work for them. The experience would be very valuable and you will most assuredly put yourself on a fast track to learning. You may even decide to pursue this end of the business and do your own sales at some point. So, definitely don't miss any estate sales.

From a buyer's perspective, if I have a choice between a garage sale and an estate sale, I check out the garage sale first. For starters, estate sales are very well advertised and a lot of people show up. There is often a long line and you end up wasting precious time standing around waiting.

Most of the people who come early are dealers and if you are the 20th person to get inside, you are looking at things that other dealers have already snatched up and will pick up later or things they rejected. That's on top of the dealers who are running the sale, who had plenty of time to check out every piece and keep the best for themselves.

I don't need all that hassle and competition and I certainly don't care to stand in line. While everyone else waits at the estate sale, I can check out four or five garage sales where there are no professionals. I go where they don't and get the deals. Garage sales are wonderful and there are no middle men. You are only dealing directly with people who want to get rid of their things...which could very well become your treasure. You have to zig while everyone else zags.

Auctions are another place to look for treasures. It would behoove you to get in the habit of checking your daily newspaper to see what's going on in the world of *stuff* being sold. I can't stress enough that your success will be determined by your mind-set. If you desire to be very successful, you have to get focused. This applies to any area of life where you wish to excel.

If you just want to make a small effort and are content with small income that's all right too, but for big results, you have to get fully involved. That means clear focus and unwavering dedication to taking the actions that will produce massive results. The more you focus the more you get, which gives you more to focus on and you continue attracting bigger and better deals.

Throughout this book, I put much emphasis on being focused, because it's truly the key to being successful. You want to get passionate about this business. I believe that once you see how much fun it is and how easy it is to create great income, you will surely be swept away.

In your everyday routine being focused means reading the ads or looking online to see if there are auctions in your area. The weekend papers usually have several auctions and depending on where you live, you should go and check them out. They will advertise several days or a week early and you want to make sure that you go to the preview.

If you are new to auctions, I would strongly advise against going on the day of the sale and placing bids before checking out everything in detail.

The preview is usually the day before and also the hours prior to the auction and you can examine everything up close. This is an important step and one not to be skipped. Write down all the items that interest you and their item numbers and after making sure they are in great condition, write down the top dollar you are willing to pay for each piece.

This is something to determine in advance and you must stick with it. Auctions are very fast paced and you can easily get caught up in the moment and spend money recklessly, which you could regret for a long time to come.

We are in this business to make a profit. It does not matter what items bring us the profit. That's why we cannot allow ourselves to get emotionally attached to anything. We buy the stuff to sell the stuff and once the price goes above our comfort zone, there is not much reason for buying it.

If something is a killer deal at a hundred dollars, is it still a killer deal at three hundred dollars? You need your money to keep doing deals, not to sit in an item that was iffy and now you have trouble selling it. We don't want our assets to become liabilities.

When something is an outstanding buy, you'll know it in your whole body and there won't be any need to second guess yourself or ask anyone else. It's smooth and flawless. With practice you will get better and better at "feeling" the excellent deals. The fabulous deals are a no-brainer, as they say.

WHERE ARE THE TREASURES?

Familiarize yourself with the auction houses in your area who conduct their auctions on a regular basis. Some of them do it weekly. Make sure you get registered. That's a process where you register a credit card or put down a refundable cash deposit and you get a bidding number. It would be wise to attend a couple of auctions, without bidding, just to get familiar with the process and get a feel for the prices.

Again, I have to remind you not to get caught up in a bidding war and overpay. This is not personal, if the other guy has to have it, let him. You have a definite purpose for being there and it could cost you dearly to get sidetracked. Even with all my knowledge, and expertise I got caught up at an auction a few years ago and foolishly spent $26,000 in one evening. I had a store at the time, so it turned out ok, and eventually I sold everything, but it was completely unnecessary and definitely not the best use of my money.

Had I spent that amount at garage sales, estate sales and moving sales, I would have gotten at least 50 times more value for my money, if not more and had a lot more fun. And possibly found some treasures that could have been worth hundreds of times more. I also took myself out of the game for a while, by over-spending and over-filling my store. So, be careful with auctions, they are just one of your many resources. There's too much competition and no time to make decisions. That's why you must buy only those things that you selected during your preview and not go any higher that the price you determined to be your comfort zone.

You have to determine prior to the auction how much you are willing to pay for each item that interests you and stick with it. There is also something called a buyer's premium which is an additional percentage that is added on to the price, along with tax so ask questions and stay on top of it.

One of my favorite methods for finding treasures used to be classified ads. I was devoted to the classified section of the newspaper and when I did that, I was tremendously successful. Once again, it's about staying focused. Amazing deals just waited for me and I would buy something and re-sell quickly and for enormous profits, very often *through the same newspaper* where I found it.

I found an ad in the Chicago Tribune once for a Cutlass Cierra from a guy who was going off to college and bought it for $1900. I turned around and put an ad right back in the Chicago Tribune and sold it for $4300 the same week.

These days classified ads have morphed into **Craigslist** postings with an added benefit; you can access them anytime and from anywhere.

The internet was certainly a game changer, but there are still some small neighborhood throw-away papers with classifieds ads in existence. Here's a tip: A lot of older people are not computer savvy, so they still list things in their local small newspapers. These people often have beautiful old things and you should definitely check into these ads. While most buyers have moved on to online classifieds only, you should explore all avenues...especially if others are playing elsewhere.

I do use Craigslist on a regular basis, to find sales and also to search for certain items or to sell

WHERE ARE THE TREASURES?

something. The key to buying from **Craigslist**, which is a giant version of classified ads, is speed. You have to get there early. In fact, you want to be the first one. You can't be first everywhere, but you can try and the Universe will reward you for your efforts.

You can't get up at 10:30 and expect the world to wait for you. Fortune does not favor the lazy. Luckily, this business offers plenty of excitement, variety and profit to keep even the laziest person interested and happy. So, start reading the ads as early as you possibly can. You want to keep the momentum going and keep yourself involved and tuned in. Just like a job requires you to show up every day and get involved in your employers affairs, so too you have to keep your attention and focus on your business.

You want to look for private sales, people who are moving or have listed items they are selling. Call the phone number, send a text, or an email (or do all three) and get the very first appointment you can. You need to get there before anyone else does. This is not one of those things where you can wait for the weekend and mosey on over when you feel like it. You have competition and they are also reading the ads.

People can't possibly list everything in their ad, so you often find great unadvertised treasures. If you see something you want, ask them if they would sell it. They may not have thought of selling that particular item, and might sell it to you very inexpensively because it's one less thing to move.

I bought a serious Hummel figurine collection once simply because I asked. This was the height of the Hummel craze and I bought them for $25 each. Some of the pieces I sold for as much as $600 dollars as well as one lamp for $1200. I don't recall the exact numbers even though I seem to have a savant-like memory when it comes to this stuff. I think I paid three or four hundred dollars and made three or four thousand, in a few weeks.

Another Hummel collection came from an insurance company through a classified ad in a small newspaper. I never got the complete story, but who cares. I got the figurines for $300 and sold them for $1900.

Another classified-ad find was three Leroy Nieman signed and numbered lithographs that I purchased for $300 and sold for $4800. My car was in the shop that day and the person who owned them was nice enough (or desperate enough) to bring them to me.

Now that we have **online auctions** a whole new world has opened up for finding treasures. Aside from eBay, there are numerous online auctions and more popping up every day. Personally, I never look at online auctions for things to resell. Remember that thousands of people are looking at the same items as you are and their bids have already more or less determined the resale value of those items.

Recently, a friend was telling me about her favorite face cream that is sold through a well-known catalog company. She said it was as good if not better than the high-end department store brands and at only $30 it's a fraction of the price. This is all good, but before ordering it, I decided to check out eBay and found it for...would you believe...$13.45, including shipping? It's the exact same item, brand new and sealed in a box, and I could have bought two and still had money left over.

WHERE ARE THE TREASURES?

This is the value of online auctions for me and prior to making a retail purchase, these days I always do my homework. Had I done this before spending $1800 on my vacuum cleaner, I would have saved myself $1300. While this may not be the best example, since most people would never spend so much on a vacuum cleaner, you will be very pleasantly surprised to discover just how much you can save by checking online auctions before buying anything retail.

I encourage you to investigate everything, including bulletin boards and again, don't disregard the neighborhood newspapers. Those small papers can be a gold-mine for finding garage sales and moving sales and private ads for things that people are selling. It's a hot-off the press treasure map.

You might want to check out **rummage sales** if there is nothing else exciting going on. I have never found anything super spectacular at a rummage sale but it only takes one time and the chances of finding a treasure there are much better than if you are sitting at home.

Let's not forget **storage auctions**. When individuals don't pay their storage fees, after a certain amount of time the contents of the unit can legally be auctioned off to the general public. Here is the tricky part: you cannot go inside to see what you are buying. All the bidders stand outside, the door is opened, and you can look in.

Everyone has the same advantage or disadvantage. What you see is what you get, unless the boxes or areas you can't see hide some great treasures. An acquaintance bought a unit for $800 and hiding behind some furniture and boxes were 2 jet-skis. Recently I heard that someone found $85,000 in cash among the junk in a storage unit. Wow-wee!

I went to storage auctions long before Hollywood made them popular and often only a handful of people showed up. On one occasion I was the only one there. I spent a whopping $25 dollars and after sneezing my way through all the dust and junk and throwing most of it out, I found a nice antique desk that I sold for $450.

It's definitely gambling and a huge amount of work, but some people find it entertaining and enjoy doing it. It may not make you rich, but you should at least familiarize yourself with this aspect of the business as well. Having said all that, in my opinion, its dirty work and you need a truck or large vehicle to cart off everything the same day, so you should hire someone to help you. To top it off, the storage facility does not allow you to throw anything away on the premises, so be prepared to take things to the dump and pay to dispose of them.

Frankly, none of these aspects appeal to me, and I don't care to dig through dusty junk, so I have not been to one of these in a long time. I don't think they are critical to your success and if you never attend a storage auction, it would have little impact on your over-all success. However, if you are interested, call the storage companies in your area and ask for a list of their upcoming auctions.

In the list of where *stuff* can be found, let's not forget **swap meets and flea markets**. These are also an excellent resource as well as a fun place to

WHERE ARE THE TREASURES?

find interesting items. I have run across some very cool things at flea markets and have made nice profits reselling these goodies. There are many people selling things at flea markets and some of them don't know or care about the value of their items, they are only interested in making a profit over what they paid for something. As is often the case, people just have too much stuff or they need the money and will sell you things for very low prices, especially if you are someone who will buy more than one item.

All swap meets are not alike, so again, you have to do some fun "work" and check out the different ones in your area. Some are weekly and sell mostly new things, so those are best to avoid. Some are once a month and all about antiques, while others have a great variety of dealers selling everything from A to Z, which is what you're looking for. Swap meets are fun and can be a good place to buy or to re-sell.

I also like to browse **consignment stores and thrift shops**. This is not a requirement, but for me it's relaxing and fun and I almost always find something fabulous. The great secret is that this business is timeless and endless and there will always be plenty of things to buy and plenty of people selling things. Don't fall into the trap of thinking that the good stuff is gone or there are too many other people doing this, or any other limiting beliefs that would prevent you from looking for treasures.

Two weeks ago I was browsing in a high-end designer clothing consignment store and found an incredible 14k gold ring for $40. There was a matching pair of sterling earrings selling for $45. It was odd that the ring was gold and the earrings were silver with gold overlay, but the set was spectacular with big turquoise stones and best of all they were selling for below the price of costume jewelry. I paid $100 for the set and sold it a few days later to another dealer for $400. Not bad!

On a return visit I found a 14K gold ring with a huge black onyx stone also selling for $40! These people are professionals...what were they doing? My point here is that you never know where you're going to find something of value. This store has been around for a long time, they sell very high-end designer clothes, they have lost of experience and should know how to distinguish gold jewelry from costume by now, yet they priced fabulous gold rings at only $40. That's crazy!

The rings were clearly marked with the 14k stamp; all they had to do was look... that's all I did. No big mystery. You will be pleasantly surprised to find plenty of opportunities like these, for they truly are everywhere all around you, on a regular basis, you just have to believe it and go find it even in the most unexpected places.

Once you tune in to the "treasure" station and stay tuned in, you will find your favorite song playing regularly...the name of that tune is K*a-ching!*

Junk shops and thrift shops can be a great resource for finding valuable items. Not long ago, I bought a $12,000 coat for $50 in a little junk store. Yes, a twelve thousand dollar coat for $50! It was a magnificent, one-of-a-kind coat, to say the least, with beads and designs that could stop traffic.

I did not even think about asking for a discount and was about to pay the $100 dollars on the price

WHERE ARE THE TREASURES?

tag, but the lady decided that I should get it for half off. My lucky day!

How did I know the value? I had seen it several months earlier at a very high-end estate sale and they were not even willing to entertain offers from the fortune they were asking for it. The story was told back then of the original price and I have no doubt this was true. Apparently they donated it for the tax-write off and somehow it ended up in this little shop…and waited for me.

When you get a little experience under your belt, you may want to place **your own ads** to let people know that you buy and you want them to call you when they sell. Until such time, there is more than enough merchandise available from the above sources.

It's a good idea to have some business cards that clearly identify what you do and make sure you give them out to everyone you meet. What exactly is it that you do? You can say that you buy estates one piece or the entire houseful… *including the house* is more accurate. You can say you buy personal property, or what you are really into is saving the planet while saving people money. You might say you are working to keep money in your community and in your country. You are doing all this and more, as I will elaborate further in these pages.

Another important factor that falls under the *where* category is the actual geographical location. It's only common sense that the better areas have the better quality merchandise.

RECYCLED ELEGANCE

No matter where you live, if you are within driving distance of wealthy neighborhoods, make it your business to go there and familiarize yourself with the area.

People who have plenty of disposable income tend to dispose of it by spending it on the finer things in life. They buy designer clothes and expensive furniture and in general surround themselves with the kind of items that are made for people in higher income brackets.

These are the individuals who purchase Mont Blanc pens and desk sets, like the one that brought me a profit of $600. They buy the Judith Lieber purses like the one I bought for a mere $5 and sold for $700. They shop at top of the line stores, like Chanel and when they part with their clothes, you can make $1,100 on a dress, like I did.

They do their shopping in high-end stores and like the woman who sold me thousands of dollars' worth of beautiful home décor items for $50, they have to get rid of the stuff just like everyone else. The big difference is the original sticker price and the quality and therefore your profit potential.

CHAPTER 5

HOW TO SHOP AT GARAGE/ESTATE/MOVING SALES

In this chapter and throughout the book I primarily use the term **garage sale** but in a broader sense I mean *any* private sale, and that includes estate sales, moving sales, etc.

If your intention is to go to sales on the weekend, you should be moving toward that end by Wednesday or Thursday. These days Craigslist is where the best ads are, but often people don't post until the night before their sale, so be sure to keep checking.

I would urge you to go to the Thursday and Friday sales if at all possible. These can be a goldmine because most people are working or they only go to sales on Saturday. This tip alone will be worth hundreds of times the price you paid for this book. You also don't want to miss the Sunday sales. There could be some phenomenal deals and the mere fact that most people don't think this way eliminates much of your competition. Once again, do the opposite of what the crowd is doing.

The advantage of Saturday is the volume. Most people hold their sales on Saturday, so you can cover a lot of them in a few hours. However you have a lot more competition, because this is the traditional garage sale day. There are no bad days and no bad sales. Neither the day, nor the area, nor the time of year, not even the lateness of the day is a determining factor. I have found jewels in not-so-great neighborhoods and even late in the day. You can't prejudge anything, you have to take the time to go and check it out.

Once you have selected which sales you will attend, you should make it a point to know exactly how you are going to get to each one of them in advance and in what order. It's important not spend precious treasure-hunting time looking for directions or driving around lost and confused. For best results, plan out in advance the most efficient way to get from one sale to the next and to the next one after that. Also have paper and pen at your fingertips in the car, because many people don't advertise in the newspaper, they just put out a sign at the corner.

I know Siri can direct you anywhere you want to go, but often at the most inconvenient moment your smart-phone becomes stupid, doesn't understand what you're saying and can't even help you find your way around the block. So, even with a GPS, it's helpful to use your time efficiently by planning out in advance the sequence of where you intend to go.

Having said all that, you're still ahead of the game if you jump out of bed Saturday morning and drive around the neighborhood, stopping at whatever sales you come across. Not ideal, but better than sleeping in.

On one occasion during a workshop in San Francisco, I had some free time on my hands and found a private sale that sounded intriguing. I wanted to check it out but we were staying in the same hotel

HOW TO SHOP AT GARAGE/ESTATE/MOVING SALES

where the workshop was and had not rented a car. No problem. I called a taxi and had him take me and wait for me. I admit that's a bit crazy but once you realize how fun and lucrative this can be you just might be that crazy too.

The cost for the cab was around $40. I only bought two things, a gold ring for $20 and a very old teddy bear which was also $20. I gave the ring to my mother and I sold the Teddy bear for $150 at an antique show several months later. Here's how my day played out in a bigger picture: my mom loved the ring, the sellers were delighted to get some cash for things they didn't want, the cab driver also made some money, the people who bought the bear were excited to have it, and I had a blast! What a great all around win-win scenario!

Taking cabs to sales is not something I recommend. However, the drive was beautiful and I still managed to turn a small profit while enjoying myself in a distant city. So much for the ridiculous idea that you have to slave away doing work you don't like just to make a few dollars. Not true!

When it comes to shopping at garage/moving/estate sales using your time efficiently is of major importance. You want to be at the first place on your list before they open. People frequently advertise 8:00 a.m. as their opening time, but will be open much earlier and you need to be there.

Saturday morning is not the time to stop for coffee or have a chat with your neighbor. You are working. This is one of the best times of the week to find treasures and you must take it seriously and have a sense of urgency.

It's a limited window of opportunity and you want to get to as many sales as possible. Make sure not to spend time browsing or rummaging through boxes of books for new reading material. Also avoid getting into unnecessary conversations during sale hours. That's for people who don't have a purpose and don't know what you know. You, my friend, are on a mission.

Garage/estate/moving sales are tremendous fun, but they are fast-paced, especially when they first open and you should save the leisurely conversation for later that evening when you can share with family or friends the fabulous stuff you bought that morning for pennies on the dollar.

For me Saturday afternoon is time for *show-and-tell*, as my friend Jim calls it. I have a blast unloading the car slowly and going through all my newly acquired treasures. I like to explain what each item is, or more importantly why I bought it and how much I paid for it. I also try things on or clean them or polish them, or find a place for them or research their values. In general it's my time to play with my new treasures. It's like I get to re-live the entire morning all over again. For me this is tremendous fun and whoever is home at the time gets to be the audience.

While I'm playing and getting acquainted with the new merchandise my brain is processing. Everything you bring into your space has to be processed and distributed so you don't get overloaded with too much stuff.

My friend, Janelle and I used to go treasure-hunting together on Saturdays for years. We always got along perfectly and had a lot of fun and on occasion we still "hunt" together. One time her granddaughter wanted to come along with us but Janelle nixed the idea, only half-jokingly, saying that she would be taking up precious cargo space! I laughed when she told me the story but I loved it and if you want to be successful this should be your mentality as well. You need to have focus and definiteness of purpose.

I once fired my boyfriend because he just wouldn't drive fast enough. When I would see a garage sale sign and urgently asked him to turn, he didn't respond quickly. We would have to go six more blocks and wait for the light, and then go all the way back. That was making me crazy, so he was relieved of his duties as Saturday morning driver. He was a maniac on the road the rest of the time, but on garage sale days he slowed to a crawl, so I think he was working on getting 'fired'. Better to be in charge of your own driving on garage sale days.

Now that you have your schedule, your sense of urgency (I said urgency, not stress) what else do you need? You need to bring cash with you. Do not expect people to take your check or hold your merchandise while you run to the bank or in any other way inconvenience them. You have to make it easy for people to do business with you and nothing is easier than cash. Between the guy who wants to pay with a check or has to leave a deposit, and one who has the exact amount, you can guess which one the sellers will favor.

Also, not helpful to show up first thing in the morning with a hundred dollar bill, because that's the same as not having any cash. Have plenty of singles, fives, tens and twenties and even quarters. One would think this is common sense, but too many times I hear people being stuck and frustrated because neither the buyer nor the seller has any change.

Put the money in your pocket, where it's easy to reach, but safe and won't fall out. Jeans are OK, but I really like cargo pants, the ones with the pockets all over and particularly the ones which have zippers on the pockets. If you buy the right ones, they are attractive and comfortable and the fabric is not as heavy as jeans. On a hot summer day, you want shorts or pants made of a light fabric. You don't have to load up the pockets with all kinds of gear and water bottles; you are not going on an African safari, just going to a few garage sales.

Also remember to dress in layers. In California it's usually cool in the early morning, but gets hot by 10 am, and it's much easier to remove a jacket than to change clothes.

Count your money before leaving the house. This is only logical, so at the end of the day you know how much you spent. I like to have $50 dollars in smaller bills in my right pocket. The rest of the money goes in my left pocket and I zip it up, so I know I don't have to worry about losing it. There is plenty of room for my cell phone, or other necessities in the other pockets.

Speaking of cell phones, please remember that it is a distraction and you are much better off leaving it in the car. I've seen people talking on the phone at garage sales and they don't even see the things they are looking at. They also tend to be loud and disruptive and people can't wait for them to leave. It's discourteous and sellers will not look at you with loving eyes as you go on endlessly about your latest drama on your phone in the midst of their garage sale. The main reason however, is that you need to stay focused on what you're doing.

It's also important to wear appropriate shoes. You don't want to be tripping over things in 5 inch platform heels or having to watch your step in uneven driveways. In my opinion sneakers are the best and certainly the safest.

I realize these are pretty basic, but very often people miss the basics. A case in point is my girlfriend Mary, who actually managed to make her way up to the Acropolis in Athens, wearing a silk dress and high heels. Climbing the ruins in Greece is treacherous enough in sneakers and having been there several times, I can tell you that truly no sane person would attempt it in heels, but the picture tells the story. There's Mary in front of the Parthenon, with the view of Athens behind her, in the middle of Greece's sweltering 110 degree summer heat, in a silk dress looking like a fashion model in full make-up and coiffed hair and wearing high heels! How she got back down remains a mystery, but clearly we just can't assume anything and even the brightest people do some perplexing things. I think I made the point of no high heels?

I also would seriously advise against carrying a purse. Either leave it at home or hide it under the seat in your car. A purse is a liability in this case and one more thing for you to keep track of.

You need your hands free and your money is already in your pocket, so unless you are going to be applying fresh make-up at every stop (which I sure hope you won't) leave the purse behind.

In fact, leave the purse, the cinnamon roll, the kids and the car-seat. You can also do without the cell phone, your iPod, the dog, the mother in law, the sandwich; anything that slows you down or distracts you, leave all that behind for these few hours.

I do not mean to assume that every person going to these sales is going to be female. Of course, all this applies to men as well, but guys already have the proper clothing and they have also mastered the idea of no-high-heels or purses at garage sales.

Here is one that also applies to everyone; put gas in your car the day before and make sure to empty it of everything that isn't nailed down. I have an Expedition that I use for garage sales and I usually have a couple of empty boxes to hold the small items that I buy along the way. You can't have things flying all over the car and getting lost, damaged or broken. It's also much easier to unload two boxes than gathering up 65 miscellaneous little things that have scattered all over the car.

If you are really ambitious, take some wrapping paper, and have it handy in case you need it. Don't expect the people who are having the sale to provide bags or boxes, or wrapping paper, or change, because they usually don't. All you need from them is a great item at a great price and you can handle the rest.

You can find paper for this purpose at any of the moving and storage facilities. It comes in a box and costs less than $10 dollars. I'm not referring to tissue

HOW TO SHOP AT GARAGE/ESTATE/MOVING SALES

paper, but rather the paper that is used for packing moving boxes.

I stay away from printed newspaper for wrapping anything. It's very messy, the ink gets on your hands as well as on your china and porcelain and clothes and you will have to spend time washing everything that was wrapped in newspaper. The ink can cause also allergies, so it's best to avoid it altogether.

Again, some of you may wonder why I'm pointing out such basic common sense concepts. Well, as the old saying goes common sense is just not that common. I have been to thousands of sales, garage and otherwise and I have seen the fallout from failure to apply common sense.

Even with all my knowledge and experience there are occasions when I forget to follow my own common sense rules and waste time correcting my own mistakes. In case you are wondering if I still go to garage sales, the answer is yes, absolutely! It's a fabulous passion and I have a wonderful time of it.

I have a lovely vintage necklace that has a magnifying glass hanging from the end of it and it serves a great purpose while looking like a nice piece of jewelry. I also have the same thing with an antique pencil at the end of it, in case I need to write something quickly. I could just have a pen in my pocket but this is more interesting and easier to use. Something else I always have with me is a jeweler's loupe. This is the little magnifying tool that jewelers use to take a very close look at a piece of jewelry.

Other necessities include a tape measure, screw drivers, a small hammer and other tools. You just never know when you need to take something apart. I was at a sale once and saw a spectacular chandelier that the owners had not even considered selling, though they were planning to completely remodel the house. When I asked about it, the man said "If you can take it down, you can have it". He was only half serious, thinking that as a woman, in heels and a short skirt, I wouldn't be removing any chandeliers. He was quite mistaken, and I ended up with a valuable crystal chandelier.

If you need glasses to read small print you must have them on you and preferably hanging around your neck. Just as you wouldn't go browsing through a bookstore without glasses, you also can't go to garage sales without them.

A word of caution here; while it is wise to check out things before you buy them please remember to use some discretion when checking markings and stamps. Try to be inconspicuous and understated; you don't need to look like a dealer.

There is a psychology here that you have to understand. Whenever people are selling things *inexpensively*, they are not looking to sell them to dealers. They are not anxious to give you a good deal just so you can turn around and make a profit. People don't want to feel like they've been taken advantage of, even if they themselves are the ones who set the prices. If you are a professional they assume that you know something they don't and if you want that item it must have some greater value that they missed.

It's different when it comes to higher priced items. Under those circumstances they welcome a dealer and understand that you have to make a profit and they are willing to work with you.

I was at an estate sale once where they had a huge amount of jewelry. I quickly picked out 12 rings that looked like they were worth more than the $5 price on each one. The house was full and there was so much to see, I couldn't stand around contemplating every ring, so I made an offer of $50 and the lady immediately accepted. I paid her and put them in my pocket. (See how convenient the cargo pants with the zippered pockets are?)

I noticed a guy standing off to the side who had grabbed a bunch of jewelry and he was inspecting each and every piece with a jeweler's loupe, obviously looking for gold.

He was about halfway through when the seller asked if he was planning on buying the pile that he had already examined. He told her no and went on to inspect the next piece while ignoring her. He made such an obnoxious production of it that one would have thought he had been sent by The Smithsonian to search out and recover the Hope Diamond.

Finally the seller had enough and in a burst of anger she went over and took everything away from him. While he stood there not knowing what just hit him, she told him in no uncertain terms that she wouldn't sell him anything. Wow, he was cut off at an estate sale. Not good.

She was upset because he wasn't giving others a chance to buy any of the 25 or 30 pieces that he had hoarded off to the side. Worse, he was taking his sweet time examining each piece and made no effort to at least put back the ones he was not planning to buy. He was holding all this merchandise hostage and other shoppers were forced to wait and see what his final decision would be.

This is a very selfish way to shop and grossly unfair to the seller. Just as this short time is our window of opportunity to find treasures, it's their limited window of opportunity to sell their merchandise. Every piece that we are hoarding in our undecided state could be bought by someone else. We have to stay conscious and aware and not hold on to things unless we intend to buy them.

I was surprised when she thrust the entire bunch into my hands and asked if I was interested in any of it. It made sense that she would offer it to me because I had just proven myself to be a no-nonsense cash buyer. This guy was not showing any sensitivity or class. The seller felt disrespected and it was her call to do as she wished. As I often say, this is not a store and there is no complaint department.

This story is a valuable illustration of a fundamental key to your success. If you learn this business the right way the first time around, you won't have to unlearn the bad habits that generate hostility and chew up your profits.

Throughout this book I keep reiterating that buyers or sellers, we are in this business together. It's the opposite side of the same coin. You cannot be in this business without experiencing both sides. If we are disrespectful of sellers, we will experience the same when we are the seller. What goes around truly comes around and it circles the globe with the speed of light. Give good deals to get good deals and be fair so you can also be treated fairly.

This blatantly greedy dealer was tying up her inventory while slowly going through each piece. Without her permission he took that entire lot off to the side and hogged it all trying <u>to see if the sellers had made any mistakes</u>. I understand his reasons, but at $5 a piece these were being sold as costume jewelry, NOT as gold.

People like him make the rest of us look bad and if it had been my sale, I would not have been favorable towards him either. Something is definitely wrong with your approach if you get thrown out of an estate sale. Incidentally, he was on the right track and when I got home I found two 18k rings, but they were in the first bunch, the ones I had already bought.

I sold the two of them for $625 and the other ones, most of which were sterling silver, I sold along the way for anywhere from $20 to $80 each. With the second batch that she thrust into my hands, she only asked me for another $50 even though there were twice as many. I bought other miscellaneous pieces that also turned out to be gold for just a couple of dollars each.

I also found a beautiful pendant at this sale that nobody had noticed and it turned out to be solid gold. I gave it to a friend as a gift and she still wears it and loves it. I paid only $2 for a gold pendant that brings joy to someone. That's fantastic!

All in all I had a very good day. Some of it came to me because I wasn't being petty. You never want to squander money but being petty can be equally detrimental.

Some clarification is in order here. If this woman had been selling the rings for $100 dollars you would do well to pull out a magnifying glass and take a very close look prior to buying. In fact it would be expected, because the price indicates that it is valuable.

Another thing I want to emphasize here is that you want to get the maximum out of every sale and do so in minimum time. This is an art that you will master, and hopefully these ideas will help you find your own groove. When you walk into a sale, regardless of inside or outside, moving, estate or garage, take a quick visual survey all around you.

I always go to the jewelry first because I love it and the potential for valuable treasures in jewelry is exciting. You never know what you can find in a heap of what appears to be junk to the untrained eye. But, you are there to see everything so just start somewhere and move quickly. If there is something that catches your attention, of course check it out, but if nothing jumps out at you, the most efficient way is to start at one end and just keep going from item to item in a row, allowing your eyes to go up one side of a table and down the other.

I completely skip all toys, strollers and all baby or child items. Even if there's some profit to be made, I have no interest in them or knowledge of prices.

I also disregard exercise equipment, because they are large and heavy. Having said that, I would have gladly bought the $1,200 Pilates equipment that I saw for $20, but it was already sold.

One area where I have a bit of a struggle is books. I love books and can easily spend hours browsing through boxes of books, but when I am focused on the big picture, I don't stop to look at books and neither should you. We don't have the luxury of browsing, when we are on a money-making mission.

Another effective method is to take a quick visual survey of the tables and then go to the items that look interesting and by interesting I mean potentially *valuable*. Do the first part quickly without stopping to handle things. There is not much point in fondling things that you are not going to buy.

That's why it's very helpful to set an intention before you leave the house. If you are looking for a coffee machine for yourself, that's fine but don't make that your major focus. You are here to find valuables that you can re-sell, and the coffee maker will be secondary. The intention keeps you focused and less likely to be distracted with things you don't need or want, while attracting to you more of what you do want.

If you get stuck on a picture frame that costs a dollar, wondering if you can use it, or whose picture you can put in it, or does it match your décor, you are wasting time. Of course if something looks promising you should grab it, immediately. Keep going don't stop to do your final evaluation. If I see a lot of great items, I start a pile off to the side somewhere and put all the things I want in that spot.

Be careful, because the minute you turn your back someone is bound to start going through your pile, so keep shopping but keep an eye on your things. Never rely on the seller to monitor your items, they are too busy and it's not their responsibility. A better way would be to have a box with you or ask if the seller has one and fill it up as you go. This is the easiest way to keep all your things intact and in one place. Keep moving and keep putting things into your box.

After you have gone through the entire sale you can stand off to the side and go through your selected items to make sure that indeed you want all of it and to make sure that's it's all in good condition. Do this quickly, it's not fair to hold on to merchandise that other people could be buying. I rarely go through the things again, I trust myself to have made good decisions the first time around and with time and experience, you will too.

If the seller's prices are high, I re-evaluate if indeed my selected items are worth it. People will almost always give you a better price when you buy in bulk. You have some negotiating power when you are buying a bunch of things, because they don't want you to put everything back and leave without buying anything.

Remember to look in the boxes and look under the tables. My $599 Vitamix was in an unopened box under a table. Nobody even noticed it and I was able to buy it for $35 dollars! I had been thinking of buying one and would have had to pay retail. Can you imagine how thrilled I was? A six hundred dollar item that I had been wanting right in front of me in a box, untouched, for $35! Just remember to look in places where other people don't.

HOW TO SHOP AT GARAGE/ESTATE/MOVING SALES

I found a box of Majolica plates once hiding under a table, which I bought for $10 and sold for $400. The $700 air purifier was in a box in the corner of the garage for $5. I bought a sterling flatware set in a dirty old box for $25 that I sold for $600. The list goes on, but I think I have emphasized the value of looking where others don't.

Some purchases are a no-brainer, and that's what we are looking for, but others may indeed require thinking on your part. When you see something that's perfect, you will know immediately and there will be no question of not buying it.

If you have to spend time contemplating how some cute but useless thing could fit into your life, you are not only wasting time but losing your focus of why you are there. Put it down and go on with your treasure hunt.

I cannot emphasize enough that you have to remember the big picture. You are not here to fill up your home with a bunch useless cute stuff, you are here to find treasures and great deals that you can turn into CASH! That's the purpose of this book to turn you into a finely-tuned treasure hunter, who can spot an opportunity from a mile away. That will take focus and thinking differently than other people and differently from the way you used to think.

It goes without saying that you will find things for yourself, your home and for your family. I am not saying don't buy it, on the contrary, you should absolutely buy it. The distinction is that you stay focused on finding things that you can re-sell and turn into cash, rather than just *spending* all your cash.

If you can sell some things and at the very least get your money back then all the things you keep for yourself will be completely free. This is where the new way of thinking comes in. Great deals and bargains are heaven, but still come under the heading of SPENDING MONEY. You have to think in terms of MAKING MONEY, if that's your first priority.

I'm not one to linger on negatives, but there is an aspect of this business that we have to get out of the way and face right now. The fact is that no matter how good you are and how much you buy or don't buy, there will be things you will regret buying and things you will regret *not* buying. On occasion you might be sorry that you brought something home and even sorrier that you left something behind.

Sometimes the other guy will get the awesome deal right in front of your nose. That's just the way it is. If you make peace with this fact of life right now, you won't have to obsess over the things that got away. It's human nature to want what we can't have. You will have plenty of successes and you must not allow yourself to dwell on something that didn't make it home with you.

My friend bought 2 small oil paintings for $8 each and sold them at auction for $2000 each. Turning $16 into $4000 is incredible by anyone's standards; however, there was one small problem. There were three paintings available at the garage sale, and by her own admission my friend was too cheap to buy the third one.

While she was thrilled by her unexpected windfall, for weeks she was upset with herself for not buying the third painting. This is called focusing on the wrong thing. You have to let it go. It was not meant to be yours. How do you know when something is not meant to be yours? It's very simple; you don't have it. If it was meant to be yours, it would be.

There are other people out there and we have to play nice and share. It feels better to let go immediately instead of fuming over your loss and kicking the tires on your car. You can put your attention on something positive and let go of the attachment to anything that you can't have. Some things have your name on it and some things have someone else's name on it. It's just that simple.

When I was younger, I would get annoyed but these days, the way I handle it is to find in myself the feeling of pleasure on behalf of the other person, and be glad for them. When I can feel happy for someone else, I invariably end up finding an even better deal down the road. When you don't allow negative thoughts to frustrate you and block your energy, you will stay in the flow and you'll find that better things show up for you. Whatever it was, you can be sure that it's not the last one of its kind on the planet.

On a few occasions I have approached people and offered them more money after they bought something I wanted and several times they even sold it to me on the spot. However, in this regard people are strange creatures; the mere fact that somebody else wants something makes them not want to give it up. I've seen it many times; a person can be debating over an item forever, not sure if they want it or not, but if someone else comes along and wants it, it almost always pushes them into buying it. An item becomes more desirable when another person wants it.

It's like the ex-boyfriend you broke up with because he was so boring and you had no feelings for him. If another woman should come along and express interest in the guy, you'll immediately see him in a different light. Wow, look out! Suddenly, he takes on a new mysterious glow and transforms into George Clooney! Amazing how the unwanted ex becomes very desirable when another woman wants him! It's human nature and it applies to *stuff* also.

Every once in a while I test this theory just for my own amusement and it's pretty solid. If I see someone unable to make up their mind about something, I tell the seller loudly enough to be overheard that if that person doesn't buy it, I will. It never fails, when they hear me, they not only make up their mind in a flash, but run over to pay immediately. It's very amusing.

This bit of psychology is worth remembering. That is; if you want something, it would serve you best to remain quiet and wait until the other person puts it down. Often people hold on to things and walk around with them, only to put most of them back the last minute. When they put something down you can pick it up, but if you express an interest while they still have it, you can be sure that you have now made that item much more desirable and you can kiss it goodbye.

If you find something that is beyond a doubt a fabulous deal and you want it, there is one way to make sure that it goes home with you: pay for it! Even if you are not finished shopping, secure that item by paying for it immediately. You are dealing with people not a department store and sometimes emotions come into play. The only way to make certain that someone won't change their mind or their spouse won't walk out the door at that exact minute and decide to keep it, is to pay for it and put it in your car.

While doing an estate sale for a client, I was listening to a woman who was still upset about a garage sale two weeks prior, where she had lost out on some treasures. She said there was a box of high-end designer purses and the man who was doing the sale told her they were $5 each.

She was complaining up a storm because while she had been looking through the box, the man got on his cell-phone and called his wife to be sure it was OK to let them go. The end result was that the fabulous purses were taken off the market, because the wife told her husband not to sell them. Ouch!

The woman was upset to say the least, to have such exciting items suddenly yanked from her grasp. To make things even more unpleasant, she decided not to give up without a fight and tried to *force* the man to sell her the purses despite his wife's decision. She explained to me that she had to make him see the error of his ways, meaning that she tried to manipulate him by laying a guilt trip on about having to keep his word! On what planet did she think that approach would work?

Two weeks later she was still complaining and asking me (a complete stranger) for agreement about how wrong the man was for not keeping his word. This is a great illustration of somebody who wasn't playing it cool.

So here's my interpretation of how it all went down: She realized that they were high-end designer purses and was (I can see it now) meticulously and endlessly inspecting the heck out of each one, much like the guy searching through the jewelry.

I know this because at my sale she was over-examining everything and asking a lot of questions that had no rhyme or reason and no purpose. She finally asked us to hold a purse which was only ten dollars, with a five dollar deposit. She said she would be back in an hour but did not return until late the following day, when once again she spent an unbelievable amount of time examining the $10 purse, as though she was seeing it for the first time.

Finally, after much talk and deliberation with another woman who came with her, she decided she didn't want the purse that she had already bought with her deposit, and asked for her five dollars back.

Some people go through life oblivious of the energy they put out and the impact their behavior has on the world around them. It was not hard to see that she must have gotten on the purse guys last nerve and most likely he only pretended to call his wife. He simply decided not to sell them to her.

This wasn't the first time I've seen someone's thoughtless behavior do them in. They remind me of the old Mr. Magoo cartoons; going through life completely clueless and never noticing the upset and chaos they leave behind. We were all tired and annoyed after dealing with this woman. When people want to post your picture at their next estate sale, in a big red circle and a red line through the center, you know your approach needs some work.

There are so many valuable lessons in this story:

HOW TO SHOP AT GARAGE/ESTATE/MOVING SALES

1. Ask questions only if they are relevant to help you to make a better decision. Let me say again, that a garage sale for people on a money-making mission, which you are, is not the social hour. Enjoy it, but don't get caught up in conversations and ask questions only as they relate to your immediate purchase. Don't allow other people's agendas to pull you into wasting valuable time. While you listen to the captivating story of how someone's grandfather worked with the Amish and learned the fine art of carving footstools, someone else is walking off with treasures at the next sale...which is exactly where you should be!

2. Move with speed and stay focused. Don't over-examine things. If you know something is a super deal...just be quiet and buy it! Even if you just found the deal of the century be cool and understated. As you rack up your success stories, you will see that good deals and great deals and phenomenal deals all require the same behavior from you. They are all fun and exciting and you don't get to jump up and down until you get home.

3. Never ask for your deposit money back when people hold something for you. Oh, this one can get ugly. A deposit is a commitment to buy and changing your mind is not an option. In the case of the woman above, she didn't even come back in an hour, as promised; she came back late the next day and no, she did not get a refund. It does not matter if it's $5 or $500. If the seller takes something off the market for you because of your commitment to buy it, it's YOURS, or you forfeit your deposit. If you're the seller, the deposit is also a commitment to sell and you don't have the luxury of changing your mind just because someone offered you more money. This is not legal advice, so please do your own research; however, honoring your word after striking a deal is a matter of ethics and good business.

Someone might ask; wasn't the guy selling the purses wrong not to sell them after quoting a price? Please hear me; no, no, no! The sellers have the right to change their mind on any item, until said item is paid for. The seller can do anything he wants with his stuff. He did not in any way owe her *his word* and when you are dealing with people you just can't have those kinds of expectations. The reality is that until an item is paid for and sitting in your car, any number of things can happen.

On the flip side, if you accidentally included your grandmother's diamond ring in the two dollar box and someone comes up to you with two dollars, are you obligated to take the money and let them walk off with your family heirloom? No, no, no! Absolutely not! Don't let anyone push you into selling something unless you really want to do so. You have every right to change your mind and say "Sorry, we made a mistake, that's not for sale". If you're not sure, hold on to it until you have a chance to think it through, rather than sell it and have pains of regret.

5. *Always have money with you*. Don't waste everyone's time including your own with silly deposits and having to go back. The inefficiency of running around is counterproductive to good business. By the time this woman drove home and drove to the bank and drove back again that $10 purse cost her more like $20 in time and gas.

6. *Don't complain*. Complaining just puts out negative vibes and ultimately nobody can undo the

past for you. To hold on to something that happened weeks ago and still gripe about it, will make anyone sick. Even if 100 million of us completely agreed with her, there would be nothing anyone could do. We have to learn to let go of the past.

7. *Consideration for others goes a long way.* If you were the only one on the planet...well, for starters, you would miss the rest of us. This lady was a good reminder that we are here as part of the whole of civilization, and we cannot act as though we are alone. It feels so good to be kind and it feels so bad to be nasty, which just goes to show that whatever we put out we are the recipients of it, first and foremost.

8. *If you find something valuable, pay for it and put it in your car.* If you find something valuable, pay for it and put it in your car. If you find something valuable, pay for it and put it in your car.

I cannot emphasize this point enough. If you think something has value and its priced right, don't hesitate, just buy it! Take a chance, spend the money and you can inspect it to your hearts content in the privacy of your own home. When I shop at these sales, I move fast and with purpose. I do not spend time lingering over labels and checking everything with a fine tooth comb. A piece of antique, a fur jacket, jewelry, a great lamp, valuable crystal, *if the price is great*, it all gets the same amount of attention. What is there to think about? Make sure it's not damaged and pay for it! Like the woman in the above example and the guy with the jewelry, we don't want to end up being the cause of our own problems.

This is something that you will master and while others are standing around vacilating, you will be on your way to the next sale. Numerous times I went and paid for something while others were standing around having lengthy discussions wondering if they should call their aunt, or what color they would use to recover it, or debating if they should go home and measure and come back later or contemplating how they would get it home, etc.

As long as something is not paid for, it's available. You are not obligated to ask other shoppers what their intentions are and then wait for their decision. The truth is most people don't know what their intentions are, or they would be acting accordingly. Don't let them hold you up. The ones who know are paying and moving on.

Some time ago at one of my sales a woman bought a stack of binders and miscellaneous paper stuff, spending exactly one dollar on the entire stack. She came back 5 hours later with one of the binders that had cost her about 7 cents and wanted to exchange it, because she had made a mistake thinking that it was an album. After I stopped rolling on the ground in hysterical laughter, I asked her if she was serious….and yes, she was!

She drove over from the next town in a brand new Lexus to exchange something that cost her less than a dime? It truly takes all kinds of people to make up this very interesting world. The key is never to take personally the crazy things people do. They're not doing anything to you, that's just the way they think and unfortunately most people don't stop to examine their thoughts and their actions. Choose to be amused instead of annoyed.

CHAPTER 6

THE FINE ART OF BARGAINING

While there truly is an art to bargaining, it's not secret mysterious rituals passed down from the merchants of the Kasbah. It's logical and intelligent principals that are based on courtesy, common sense, and class (the three C's). The following tips and techniques are so valuable they could be a book all by themselves. These techniques will serve you well in this business and are fundamental to your success. While I write most of the chapter addressed to "*you*", it is not to imply that any of my wonderful readers would be inclined to do the things that I caution against. It's simply for ease of expression that the word "you" is used.

Perhaps the best secret of a great bargainer is to know when NOT to bargain and what NOT to do.

For starters, I would seriously advise you **not** to bargain on something that is already an awesome deal. This is where **common sense** comes in. I have seen people unthinkingly deprive themselves of something they really wanted that was incredibly priced by attempting to get an even better price. If it's already a fantastic deal what were they trying to accomplish?

If you do this the seller may start re-thinking the whole thing and change his mind. I've seen it happen to others and in my early days, I saw it happen to me.

Ouch! The only reason you are buying the item in the first place is because it's priced right, so attempting to manipulate the numbers further is not worth the risk of killing the deal.

Sellers have been known to get upset when they perceive someone is pushing at them from a greedy perspective. I have seen people become irate and insulted when someone offered what they considered to be an offensive price. If a seller tells you he would rather eat it, burn it, or throw it away, you can be sure the negotiations have taken a downhill turn and are about to come to a screeching halt.

There may be a time or two that someone will give in, but even if they do, you will not feel very good about the whole thing. There are so many deals out there, its bad business and bad karma to take advantage.

There have been times that an item was so ridiculously underpriced that I actually gave someone more than they were asking. I certainly don't make a habit of this and I'm not saying you have to do it, but sometimes it makes sense and it just feels right.

When you are generous it makes you feel good and the Universe will be generous with you. So please no ridiculous bargaining on great deals. I have been on both sides and have experienced just about anything you can think of and that's why you bought this book.

And please don't even think about bargaining on anything that's priced under a dollar. Don't ask if you can have it for a dime instead of a quarter...that's just

THE FINE ART OF BARGAINING

being cheap and it's the wrong mind-set if you are looking to create wealth. What goes around comes around and if you are stingy with your sellers you can be sure that your future buyers will be stingy with you. You want to keep that good energy flowing by having a generous spirit. What are you doing buying something for less than a dollar anyway?

Another characteristic of an excellent bargainer is extending respect to the people you are buying from. This is where **courtesy** comes in. Whatever you do, don't whine and don't plead. Don't put on a sad face or tell sad stories to make people feel sorry for you in order to get a better price. That's very unattractive and I can guarantee you that you will thwart your success if you try to manipulate people's emotions.

Just last week I was browsing at a sale watching two women turn a pleasant day into a nightmare for the seller with their bargaining methods. Every time she gave them a price they countered...I mean she said four dollars and they said two. She said a dollar, they said 50 cents. She said there was nothing at her sale priced less than a dollar... they said 50 cents again, as though she hadn't even spoken. Again, she said no. Then they tried bunching things together and getting her to throw in free stuff. It was simultaneously comical and aggravating to watch. Every time they didn't get their way they said something to each other in a foreign language. The seller was clearly losing her cool but they didn't notice or care. Finally when she turned down another insulting offer, the women whose new Mercedes was parked 10 feet away countered by saying *"You have to give it to me...because I don't have money!"* Wow...that qualifies as the worst bargaining line in history! It wasn't money she was missing...it was courtesy, class, common sense and...my book!

I had seen these two in action at other sales and every time they left behind angry sellers vowing never to have another garage sale again as long as they live.

An even less attractive and very immature method is to grind on the seller. This is when adults act like whiny little kids and keep bugging and nagging hoping someone will finally give in. This behavior is left over from childhood and has no place in the adult world.

This strategy may have worked at age 6 with parents who would finally give in to the relentlessly badgering child, but when a full-grown adult uses it to get their way, it is seriously annoying. People who are inclined to act like a 6 year old shouldn't be surprised when grownups around them lose their patience and become unpleasant. It's so important to maintain a professional and friendly demeanor and conduct ourselves with **class**.

A number of years ago I owned a designer-consignment boutique and I had a customer who was trying to get a better price by grinding me endlessly about a blue silk dress. I explained to her that I would be losing money if I sold it for her price and that I had absolutely no intention of doing so, but she kept following me all over the store whining and pleading to get her way. She figured that eventually she would wear me down and I would give in. This woman was oblivious to the fact that I was getting very annoyed with her and she completely ignored me when I told her to leave.

THE FINE ART OF BARGAINING

If something isn't working doing more of it isn't going to work any better. How thick headed can someone be not to notice that they are not getting their desired outcome? She kept on with her routine until I finally lost my patience and grabbed the dress out of her hands and ripped it right down the middle. Then I shoved the tattered pieces back into her hands and pushed her out the front door. Yikes!

Admittedly, it was not one if my finer moments but she simply wouldn't stop and I had reached the end of my patience. My mother however, who witnessed the whole thing thought it was hysterical and referred to my "blue-silk-dress moment" often. The family got a lot of laughs out of it, but I'm sure the woman who found herself unceremoniously tossed out didn't think it was amusing. Hopefully that episode cured her of that nasty bargaining habit, but I doubt it. This was clearly not her first time and occasionally she probably got her way.

Even if we are successful in grinding people down and they give in, there will be a lot of negative, hostile energy coming our way and that is not the path to riches. Bargaining is very much like sales, never to be taken personally. What distinguishes a truly good sales person is the ability to listen and that means getting out of their own agenda and caring about how their words are landing on the other person.

To be successful, we are looking to have win-win situations. This is a powerful, wealth-making business and although every deal in itself is important it's the string of deals that gives you momentum and allows you to build a successful career. One sure way to keep grounded is to stay detached. There is nothing out there that you must have. If the price is wrong, it's not worth it, if the price is right, just buy it.

I had an appointment once with a man who had a business next to my store. His wife died a few years earlier and he wanted to clear out her things. We finally came to an agreement after a very lengthy negotiating session, in which I stuck to my offer. The next day he came to my store and left a message telling one of the girls that he wanted to take me to dinner...he was so impressed with the fact that I out negotiated him. He said he'd had a successful business for decades and was used to winning in negotiations and couldn't figure out how I got my way.

The truth is that I got my way because I wasn't attached to getting my way. I was pleasant and having fun and enjoying the game. Whether I got the stuff or not, I didn't care....it was only worth it to me at my price. Rather than having hard feelings or regret, he was amused and impressed because there was no manipulation on my part...only detached interest.

Another costly mistake to avoid is making ridiculous and insulting offers. If the price is $25 don't offer $3. Some people throw out offers without even thinking. Also remember, not to make offers unless you are serious and intend to honor it.

Some buyers have a most obnoxious habit of cutting every price in half, regardless of what price you give them. This is definitely not a well-thought out bargaining method either. If you keep the three C's in mind while bargaining, you will prosper quickly in a happy and healthy way.

Another aspect of **courtesy** is simply a matter of being respectful to the sellers. Don't start by devaluing their merchandise and pointing out every dent and scratch, or *issues* as I call them. Grant it, the item may have several *issues* but sellers are not blind and you don't need to alienate them by pointing out the negatives right away. Unless you find something they were not likely to have noticed, people often take these things personally and it will not be beneficial to you to build your negotiations on negative aspects.

One of my personal pet peeves is people wanting a better price because they need to have something altered or re-upholstered to match their personal requirements. Please don't use this argument to bargain because it doesn't have anything to do with the item itself. How is it the fault of the seller that the green on his chair doesn't match your couch? A spot that needs cleaning is a valid point, because everyone would have the same requirement. However, if you need to have something shortened, that is completely your problem and has nothing to do with the value of that item.

I am not suggesting that you don't consider all your expenses when buying something because indeed you should. I **am** saying that it's not the seller's concern. The only reason people throw these things out there is because they want a better price. We all understand this but when you try to make your problem the seller's problem, he will not appreciate you painting him into a corner. Truly, nobody cares how or why you came up with your offer. They don't want someone's story...they just want to sell their stuff.

Also remember that nothing will destroy the negotiations faster than getting into an argumentative mode with the seller. You may be right but you will go home empty handed. Once again, **common sense** says that if you take an oppositional position people will give the item to the dog before they give it to you. If you don't want to have a blue-silk-dress experience, never, ever argue with the sellers about anything. You're not there to set them straight, you are actually both looking for the same outcome...you want to buy something and they want to sell it.

I went to visit a friend once, who has a fabulous consignment store and has owned her successful business for several decades. She obviously knows what she's doing and has not only excellent taste, but great business sense.

When I walked in, there was a noisy woman with lots of attitude, looking at a collection of gold charms with a $250 price tag and complaining because my friend would not separate the collection for her and sell only the ones she wanted.

My friend kept her cool even after the woman told her in a very loud and offensive voice that if it had been her shop she would indeed be selling the charms separately. When this had no effect, she asked my friend to give her the very best price for the set.

After my friend gave her the *bottom price* which was only $200, she proceeded to make an offer of $150. After that was turned down, she proceeded to storm out of the store in a deeply offended huff!

This entire exchange was ugly and uncomfortable and completely unnecessary. The woman was rude and insulting and those are interestingly enough, often the individuals who act like they've been insulted! Personal ego should never be brought into negotiations and telling people how they should run their business or their sale is offensive and counterproductive to say the least. The key here is to recognize that we are on the same side as the seller, not to put ourselves in an oppositional position, like we have to conquer the other side. There is no other side...we all respond to nice people and are turned off by unpleasant rude behavior.

Now, let's get down to the bargaining methods that will contribute greatly to your success. These valuable techniques will have people inviting you back, wanting to do business with you again and again.

Number one rule; don't be the first one to quote a price. I learned this a long time ago, but truly it's just common sense. Once a number comes out of your mouth, it's impossible to take it back…..you can't un-ring a bell, as they say. Most sellers have a dollar figure in mind, but don't want to express it, hoping your offer will be higher. That's exactly the reason you don't want to say a price first...you don't want your offer to be higher than what the seller has in mind.

After we go back and forth and I ask how much they want and they ask how much I would pay, I end it all by saying, in a very light and humorous way "Look...I'm used to buying things inexpensively, so you can't be expecting me to throw out some big number, just tell me what you have in mind". This can intimidate people a little, as their high hopes of big dollars clash with the reality of a *cheap* buyer. This line has always worked for me, especially because I say it with humor, otherwise we just dance back and forth with both of us waiting for the other to throw out a number.

I went to a sale once at a very high-end home where truly everything was off the charts expensive. I started putting things in a pile even though the prices were quite high. I loved the quality and uniqueness of the many beautiful things I was selecting. I was strictly shopping for myself and knew I was well into several hundred dollars buying things that I didn't need but I was on a roll. Soon I had a humongous pile and by my rough estimation I was well over a thousand dollars when I finally asked the woman to total my purchases.

She looked at the pile and said *"How much do you want to pay?* My response was *"As little as possible."* She stood for a second surveying my gigantic collection and said: "How about $50 for everything?" *How much!? Was she kidding?* I was stunned and paid her as rapidly as my hands could fish the money out of my pocket. I thought any minute she's going to snap out of it and come to her senses but the truth is that she was so happy to get rid of all the stuff she no longer wanted, that she was hoping **I** wouldn't change **my** mind!

To ask only $50 for thousands of dollars' worth of incredible stuff is the equivalent of giving it away, and I was in complete amazement. Because I had no way of knowing what price she had in mind, I just kept my mouth shut and let her speak first. I was prepared to pay at least six hundred dollars, but all she wanted was fifty. Even if you have to bite your tongue, never make an offer first.

THE FINE ART OF BARGAINING

My $50 purchase filled my Expedition. After I quickly loaded everything, I continued to shop knowing that the price tags were just decoration. She wanted to be free of the stuff and her husband wanted to get his 3-car garage back. That was a fabulous day and an incredible sale and I had so much fun buying gorgeous things for pennies on the dollar. One of my favorite pieces was a bronze monkey candle-holder, which I still treasure, with the $295 price tag still on the bottom. I held on to many of those beautiful things and still enjoy them. I also sold some of them, and even gave some as gifts. The few items I sold not only paid for my purchase, but for all my purchases for the entire month. As a side note; many people came to that sale expecting garage sale prices and left without buying anything, because they were put off by the prices. That was perfect for me, because I was willing to pay more and the bigger my pile got, the more likely the seller was to negotiate with me.

So many lessons I can pass on from this sale: For starters, you can never go wrong with high-quality items. As soon as you can afford it, seek out and invest in the good stuff. One of the things included in my $50 purchase was an exquisite Maitland-Smith bronze monkey toilet paper holder, new in a box, which I sold on eBay for $275. That's a $225 profit and I still had an Expedition full of high-end goodies. If you have the finances, be willing to invest it in your business. I was willing to pay $600 for the lot, because it would still have been a bargain.

Don't be concerned about other people's 'garage sale' mentality. Meaning; some people think *garage sale* equals give-away prices and they run when things are priced outside of their comfort zone. This is great for the rest of us serious shoppers. Even at my sales once in a while someone will act indignant because my prices are too high for them. Who cares? Those are not the customers I'm cultivating. They actually believe that by acting huffy, someone will feel bad and reduce their prices to their liking. That's just another bargaining technique that never works.

Here is another golden tip: If you want to make a counter offer after the seller gave you a price, it helps to say something like "It's a nice piece but my offer would be xx dollars. And then you add the phrase…"*that's the amount I can pay*" or you can say "*that's as high as I can go*". Or, I sometimes use the phrase "*that's all it's worth to me.*"

In a way, you are sympathizing with the seller, by agreeing that it's an attractive piece, but you can only spend so much. This is a very elegant strategy because you are not trying to knock the item; you are merely speaking **your** truth. When you say "*that's all it's worth to me*" or "*That's the amount I would be willing to pay*" or "*that's 'the maximum I could pay*" you take out anything personal and since nobody can argue with "*your truth*" the ball is back in the seller's court. Now they have to decide whether or not to accept your price.

You would be surprised by how frequently your offer is accepted! Even if it's declined a new price point has been introduced and the negotiations start all over again from the price you just offered.

This part is important enough to repeat and give you an example. Let's say you are looking at a sofa and your sellers are asking $800. Sometimes people

THE FINE ART OF BARGAINING

are unrealistic about how much to ask and they simply pluck numbers out of thin air.

You may think they are crazy but it would not endear you to them to suggest that they get a reality check. Your job is to decide exactly how much **you** would be willing to pay. Once you have that figure, offer a little bit less, so you have some wiggle room. If your maximum price would be $350, you would offer $250 or 300 at the most. You would simply say that the sofa is very nice but it's only worth $250 **to you**.

I never-ever use the word "afford". The difference between "*not being able to afford something*", and "*determining how much you are willing to spend on it*" is huge, gigantic, enormous!

The first one makes you sound weak, like a victim, and we all want to avoid victims. The second one makes you sound like you know what you are doing and you are coming from a position of strength.

In fact, never use the phrase "*I can't afford it*". It's very dis-empowering and you should consider eliminating it from your vocabulary and your life, completely. Successful people don't think or speak that language. Your subconscious is always listening and you don't want to re-enforce such negative phrases.

Back to the sofa and your offer; you have not offended anyone, and you're still in the game. Now that your sellers are presented with your $250 offer, it could go one of several ways; they could say no they would rather chop it up and use it for firewood, or they could say yes, when can you pick it up, or they could make a counter offer.

This is where the negotiations take a very interesting turn, so pay close attention: Their counter offer is now based upon your $300 offer and **not** on their original asking price. At this point their original price is no longer in play and now they have to decide what to do with your offer. Your $250 offer is a very clear indication that you won't pay anything close to their $800 asking price. Your $250 ball is now in their court. That's how you can buy the sofa that was originally eight hundred for three hundred or less.

A few months ago, I bought a $6,225 Henredon dining table and two $1495 leather dining chairs (yes, I did my research to find the original retail prices) all for a total of $320. I didn't even realize they were made by Henredon, a manufacturer of fine high-end furniture until we were picking them up. It was simply a beautiful set, even at the $600 asking price. The sellers had it in the garage in a huge ocean-view home and they wanted it gone. It was a garage sale and a woman was hovering over it, asking the owner to take measurements and promising to come back later. I took one look and offered $300 and we agreed on $320. The deal was done in less than two minutes. Having it turn out to be a great brand name was a tremendous bonus. I sold the leather chairs for $900 for the pair and the table to a different buyer for $1500. My prices were great, considering the original retail and the high-demand value of the brand. Both buyers were very happy and I was delighted with the $2,080 profit.

If you can't agree on a price that suits you, it's time to leave. In this business, you don't want to get attached to any particular deal. Leave your phone number with your offer and go on to the next one.

When buying personal property from private individuals, don't pay too much attention to the prices. It's only a starting point and if you have a motivated seller the price may not mean much.

I once bought an entire houseful of incredible high-end furniture for a quarter of the price that the seller was asking for the bedroom set alone! I loved this seller because he was cool and had great taste. He was a young guy who had made a lot of money in the dot-com craze and had furnished his condo with expensive, beautiful things. His dream was to go to the famous Cordon Bleu culinary school in Paris and now that he had the financial means nothing was going to interfere with his dream.

He ran a classified ad in the local paper with a partial list of items and the prices he was asking. His prices were very high, but I called him anyway and asked if he was negotiable. Because he had listed his high prices in the ad, he did not get much of a response and I think he was starting to worry that he wouldn't get any buyers, which would delay his move to Paris.

He had a gorgeous Thomasville bedroom set with the bedding and the mattress he had purchased for $12,000. He had his list printed out and was asking $5,000 just for the bedroom set.

Everything in the place was tasteful and expensive. There was a floor lamp that he purchased for $600 and he was asking $250 for it. I still have that great floor lamp because after some fun negotiating I ended up buying the contents of the entire condo.

Although he was asking $5,000 for the bedroom set alone, would you believe I was able to buy everything for $1700? Sometimes it's just that insane!

I sold the bedroom set for $4,300 and sold the other items for equally great profits. You never know what to expect, so don't write anything off before you check it out. He was very motivated and the biggest motivating factor for him was that I would buy all of it, pay cash immediately and get it all out quickly.

Money was definitely not his main consideration. His problem was getting rid of a house full of stuff he no longer wanted and I solved his problem. Not only was I very happy, but after we concluded our deal and I got everything out in an expedient manner as promised, he called me up and thanked me. He was a class act and every buyer's dream.

When you understand that frequently it's not about the money you will be able to work with people and help them to solve their problems. There is a popular quote from the even more popular motivational speaker Zig Ziglar that says "*You can have everything you want in life, if you help other people get what they want*" If you can give others what they want, they will give you what you want and you will prosper.

The best way to negotiate a good deal is to **find out why people are selling** and to see if you can help them. Often the motivating factor is space. People want new furniture and they need the old stuff gone. Moving and downsizing always involves things that have to go. For many individuals their number one concern is not how much they can get, rather how quickly you can get something unwanted out of their life.

When I'm in someone's home and looking at a larger purchase, I always ask why they are selling. That's my first question. I ask because it may determine the rest of the negotiations. Your best deals come from "motivated sellers". They are the ones who make this business so lucrative. A motivated seller is someone who is selling for reasons other than money. I was honest in telling my dot.com guy up front that I would not pay his prices and he was honest in telling me that he was willing to talk.

Again, let me say that even though one might imagine that money is number one on everyone's priority list, it's absolutely not so. Many if not most sellers don't care about the money as much as they care about some other goal they are trying to meet and the items in questions are now simply in the way.

While motivated sellers are just about the best, there is another category of sellers that's even better. These are the ones I call **negligent sellers**. They just don't care what something is worth or how much they get for it. These are the people who never return things to the stores; they simply toss them into the closet and forget about them for months or years. They buy expensive things probably as retail therapy and often never use most of the things they buy.

Some people simply love to spend money and spend it often... and they don't much care what happens to the stuff after the shopping part. Much like the lady recently at a local garage sale, who was selling cashmere sweaters for 50 cents, the same price she was asking for old t-shirts. It made no sense at all, but I was not about to argue with her. I bought all 8 of them for $4.00. She even told me they were cashmere and two of them were brand new with price tags. She paid over $100 for most of them just a few months earlier. Surely, she could have given them away as gifts...who wouldn't appreciate a cashmere sweater? She spent over $800 just to give it all away for $4...that's a little crazy, but thank you very much!

Isn't it taking advantage if someone is selling things way below their value? If someone has priced a diamond ring for $5 what should you do? Only one thing; buy it! As I say repeatedly throughout this book: It is not our job to point out to sellers that they could get more. It's their job to do the minimal research to ascertain the value of their property. Our job as the buyer is to buy and their job as the seller is to sell. If people are negligent and don't care enough to act in their own best interest, it is not up to us to educate them.

When it comes to inheritance, people seem to care even less. I went to a private sale once from a classified ad. The house was a grand old house once upon a time but it had been neglected for years and looked like it could fall over if someone sneezed hard. The story was that the woman who owned it had passed away and left half to the church and half to her brother. I was dealing with the brother who was trying to sell the contents of the house. I was poking around in the mess when he said he needed to leave but told me to stay and keep looking and he would be back in an hour.

THE FINE ART OF BARGAINING

He even gave me some boxes to fill up in case I found things I wanted. I was searching in one of the bedroom drawers having a great time, when I found a bunch of gold jewelry. There was a beautiful heavy 14k pocket watch with a thick gold chain, along with eight or nine other fabulous gold pieces. I put everything in the box and kept going. By the time he came back I had filled up all three boxes and then some. When I asked how much he wanted for everything, he barely glanced at the boxes before he said $30. As I stood there dumb-founded, he was already in the kitchen making a sandwich. I paid the $30, took my boxes and left.

So what had just happened? I got thousands of dollars' worth of jewelry along with a bunch of other valuable items for thirty bucks?? What happened was that I was dealing with a negligent seller. Someone who didn't even take the time and trouble to lean down and look at the things I had accumulated in the boxes.

He had been staying in the house for several months and never bothered to search the drawers? He let a complete stranger go through the stuff without doing so first. Not to sound ungrateful, but seriously….how negligent can you be? I was not about to clue him in that he should charge me more because there was jewelry in the boxes. For goodness sake, all he had to do was look!

Believe it or not, this has happened far too many times to count it as a fluke. I have even bought piggy banks that obviously had money inside….you could hear the coins hitting the dollar bills. Instead of selling it to me for a dollar, they could have thrown it against the wall and picked the money off the floor. Yes, indeed, some of us are quite negligent.

Another important aspect for anyone aspiring to be an excellent bargainer is to master the skill of establishing *rapport*. This may be the most valuable part of your bargaining skills, as it relates to unconscious human interaction. My favorite description for the word *rapport* is "*A feeling of comfort and connectedness between people*" If connecting doesn't come naturally for you, work on being friendly and interested. People are more likely to do business with people they like.

I find it infinitely fascinating to see how different individuals live, how they decorate, what reasons they have for selling, etc. Because I take an **honest** interest, people tend to feel comfortable with me. No matter who I am speaking with, there is always some small thing I can find that we have in common.

Even though you are there to conduct business, if you show some *genuine* interest you can be sure it will be appreciated. Over the years, I have listened to stories galore and looked at countless family pictures. Nothing is all business and in the people business it's vitally important to establish a connection.

It's the connection that has people inviting you back. If someone feels comfortable with you, they will continue to do business with you. Many times I gave an offer and people called me back and chose to do business with me, in spite of a higher offer from someone else, simply because they liked me and trusted me. I strive to be genuine and the fact that I take a true interest goes a long way. As I keep saying…..it's really not all about the money.

THE FINE ART OF BARGAINING

We all get "vibes" from others and sometimes just being in the presence of someone rubs us the wrong way without knowing why. In this same way people will get a "sense" or a feeling about you and that feeling is what dictates to them if they can trust you or not. When you are in someone's home you are on their turf and they are even more alert. If they trust you and like you, they will do business with you, it's really that simple. I have had ongoing relationships' for many years and an enormous amount of referrals because people know that I am fair and they feel comfortable in recommending me to their friends and even to their parents and other relatives. That is very high praise indeed and well worth everything it takes to earn it.

Through the years I have been in hundreds, if not thousands of homes and have met thousands of people and I'm happy to report that 99% of my experiences have been positive. I've helped people solve decorating problems and often took the time to move things around to make someone's house more attractive or easier to sell. I have referred and arranged for handy-men, plumbers, painters, maid service, movers, etc., simply because someone needed it.

Once after concluding some deals with an elderly gentleman, I went over to his new place and hung all his pictures. I took a girlfriend with me and we had the best time doing something that for us was easy and fun but for him was huge and overwhelming. He was so happy and grateful to have the caring and attention, that when it was all done and looking beautiful, he brought out a bottle of champagne, got down on his knees and asked me to marry him! What a sweet moment and surely worth a few hours of my time to make someone happy!

I'm not suggesting you stay for the weekend, do the laundry and fertilize the lawn, but truly you can never go wrong by giving. I've had many invitations to dinners and parties and events and dates and met some wonderful people and made great friends along the way. Two of my best friends are garage sale treasures. I met them while shopping at their garage sale. One of them has been my dearest friend for 26 years. You truly never know what treasures you'll find at garage sales!

Something else I'm in the habit of doing, is asking sellers how much they paid for an item. Most often, they will be happy to tell you. Sometimes they even produce the original receipt. It helps in making your decision but it's not necessary. You are doing quick turn-around sales and providing pedigree and original cost is not an issue under those circumstances.

If you decide to buy high-end items and expensive art, original receipts will be very helpful. Right now you just want to earn as you learn. Asking the seller for the original cost of an item helps you determine if you have any interest. If the seller tells you the dining room set cost $800 retail, and he wants $600 there is obviously no room in that deal to make a profit. It's unrealistic on their part to expect to recover 75% of the money that was spent on an average piece of furniture. No need in educating them...just go on to the next deal.

If you look at the numbers this is how it plays out: If the original price was $800, it's unlikely that you would get more than half, or $400 if you resell it, and

THE FINE ART OF BARGAINING

that means you want to pay no more than $200 to have enough room to feel comfortable. The other factors are this: dining rooms are not high demand items, you will have to store it somewhere until it sells and you need a vehicle big enough to transport it. Even at $200 I would pass on the deal. There are so many other exciting bargains out there, why drag a dining room set around just to see if you can make $200?

Sellers often hope to recover half of what they paid for an item, but that doesn't work for you either. If you pay them half of retail, where in the world is your profit? This might be a half-way decent deal for someone who actually needs a dining room set, but for you as a dealer, who needs a **profit**; this formula is a recipe for losing money. As I've said repeatedly... there are too many fabulous, no-brainer deals to waste time and money on the iffy ones.

If the dining set was part of a package deal and you could buy it for $50....now we're talking! I love buying many items in a package deal and rarely even waste time to go look at just one thing. You want to buy a houseful of stuff for obvious reasons....the more you buy the better the price.

Here is a formula you might use for determining how much to pay. Let's say you're looking at 8 items. Furniture or décor or costume jewelry, or designer clothes, applies to most buy-the-whole-lot deals. I try to determine realistically how much I can resell 2 of those items for and that's pretty close to the max I'm willing to pay.

Here is a simple example: 8 pieces of costume jewelry, the seller wants $200. If I think I can sell 2 of them for $50, I would pay $50. This is not a hard and fast rule and it's certainly not etched in stone, in fact, far from it. It's merely a guideline until you can establish something that feels right for you. If I can recover the $50 from the first 2 pieces than the rest is all profit.

You don't want to chase after your money and worry about how you will make it back. There has to be plenty of profit potential otherwise it's just not a good deal. In this example I am averaging my prices for re-selling to be $25 each. If I buy this lot for $50, and re-sell each piece for $25 I will make $150 profit.

The only problem here is that the seller is not asking $50, he's asking $200. That's why I said it doesn't matter what people are asking, what's important is what **you** are willing to pay, and that's based on your estimation in what you can re-sell the items for. If the seller just plucked his price out of thin air, which often is the case, you can offer $40 or $50 for the lot.

If you get up to $75, you're paying too much because now you have to sell 3 pieces just to get your money back, before you see any profit. Now you have 5 pieces left and if you get $25 for each of them over time, you will have made $125 profit….not a big deal at all.

The ideal price for all 8 pieces would be $20 dollars. I would consider this an average deal and not one to jump up and down about, but it's good enough to turn a profit and keep you going. Deals like this will be your bread and butter and luckily they are abundantly available. It's fun and interesting and it adds up quickly to create a lucrative income stream. I would rather spend $100 dollars and buy a bigger collection. Unless you resell them in one batch to a dealer, chances are the pieces will be tied up in your inventory, so tie up only small amounts of money.

Last year I found a $700 air cleaner for $5.00. I have one of these already and hate to admit that I paid retail for mine a few years earlier. I found this one at an estate sale in the garage. Someone had taken it apart to clean it but all the parts were there in the box. I couldn't waste time putting it together and testing it, I was willing to take the $5 gamble to do that at home. It turned out to be almost brand new and working perfectly, so that was a fabulous deal.

I sold it on eBay for $295. If I wanted $400, it would take a little longer and for $500 even longer and certainly more work. At $295 I made a $290 profit and that was plenty for me to turn it over and go on to the next thing. I don't try and get top dollar for everything. I am interested in volume and I know that keeping it all circulating is the best way to create momentum and ever increasing Income.

The point here is that a $5 risk is not really a risk if the resale potential is several hundred dollars, but a risk of several hundred dollars is an entirely different ballgame. Buying every-day items such as furniture that's currently selling will only be profitable if the acquisition price is ridiculously low. If that air cleaner had been one of those $50 retail items, it would not have made sense to spend $5 to see it if it works, because even if it did, it has no resale value.

I once found a shoebox full of little miniature metal carved figurines. Each piece was very detailed, in an elegant box like fine jewelry and each box had a retail sticker price between approximately $20 and $100 dollars. I paid a total of $20 for all of them and had no clue of what I was buying.

The fact that the prices added up to several hundred dollars and the packaging of each item made it seem like it would be an interesting deal for a mere $20. After a bit of research (pre-internet days) I found that my "Goebel Miniatures" were highly sought-after collectibles. After about 10 phone calls, I had found a buyer through a collectors club and I was on my way to deliver the goods. We had agreed on a price in the form of **cash only** and I said I would be more than happy to drop it off. I was happy to deliver it because the buyer was waiting for me with $7800 cash!

These deals are so exiting and so incredibly rich that it keeps you in love with this business. I grant you they don't happen every day, but you also don't have to risk high amounts of money on mediocre deals. You simply have to keep going and keep looking.

When I was teaching in seminars all across the country, I used to say that every day won't be a *doll-day*, but there are so many incredible days that will blow your mind and re-energize every cell in your body and your finances. I haven't seen anybody jump up and down when they open their weekly paycheck, but I have certainly done the happy dance more times than I can count!

CHAPTER 7

SELLING YOUR TREASURES FOR MEGA PROFITS

It's wonderful to come home with fabulous bargains but in order to have a successful business; you have to turn these goodies into cash. The following may sound too simplistic for those that like to keep things complicated, but one of the best ways to generate instant cash is...you guessed it...a garage sale. As I mention in other parts of this book; a garage sale is one of the best places to find incredible items and I'm here to tell you that it's also one of the best ways to sell things and create *immediate income.*

Some people have been turned off by garage sales because their previous experiences failed to make money, but I've dedicated an entire chapter that outlines in detail how to organize and pull off seriously *profitable* garage sales.

That's exactly how I started and for anyone new to this, it's still the best place to start and one of the fastest ways to generate instant cash. My first sale came about because I had accumulated a bunch of things and I thought that other people might be interested in buying them. I displayed it all in one room and put an ad in the paper. I spent a total of maybe $200 throughout the summer on all the things from various garage sales.

I had no idea what kind of a response to expect from the ad and was thrilled when the first guy paid me $200 in cash for a few things...now I had recovered all my expenses. The next person didn't buy anything, but the third was a couple who may be partly responsible for my career and the fact that I'm sitting here writing this book.

They were about to open a shop and wanted to buy everything I had! I was asking $1500 and they only wanted to pay $1000, but we finally agreed on $1200. Was I ever excited! I was in my late teens at the time and I was completely hooked! Why in the world would I get a job, to which I was highly allergic, when I could make lots of money and have fun doing this?

As far as opportunities go, there are just as many now as there ever were. I truly knew nothing when I started, I had no mentors, nobody to guide me and certainly no how-to-books on the subject. My family members were quite amused and teased me about my garage sale habits. Eventually they realized that I was making more money *playing* than they were making working, and the teasing turned into a kind of dumbfounded respect.

"So, where do you sell the stuff?" This is one of the most frequent questions people ask me. If you look at this as a real business, you will have to familiarize yourself with how the *stuff-market* works. The internet has made it very easy to research values and find buyers. When I started, it was infinitely more challenging to find buyers for the things I wanted to sell.

There are only three questions you need answered. What do you have? What is it worth?

SELLING YOUR TREASURES FOR MEGA PROFITS

Where can you sell it for the highest possible dollar amount? There is an overwhelming amount of information available on any given subject, such as antiques or furniture or collectibles or watches or books or art...pick a subject and it comes with endless information.

When I searched Google for the word **vintage,** there were exactly 153,000,000 responses. Wow!

It's not necessary to get an education. Learning about antique furniture alone would be a daunting task to master. If you focus your energies on learning about things you have not yet come across, you are wasting your time. While it's very helpful to know a little about everything, that's all you need to know...a little bit can take you a long way.

I said before that I didn't know the value of the dolls before I bought them; it just seemed like a good deal. I also said that I don't specialize in anything,....**except making money**.

There are countless publications, online newsletters and endless number of organizations and clubs dedicated to the things they are passionate about. When you have something you want to know more about...start researching it.

There really is no need to go out and gather information or make great efforts to familiarize yourself with things that have no relevance at the moment. Other people might disagree, but in my opinion you don't need to over-educate yourself, you just need to get out there and start doing something. To make life easier, I would recommend a computer, but these days most people have one, so that's no longer a big deal. If I'm looking at something that I'm not sure about, I often do a discreet search on my iPhone to help me make a better decision.

For now we want to begin by getting our feet wet and creating immediate income by having a garage sale. Start by going through every room in your home, every closet, and pull out all the things that you are no longer using. Americans have more junk...sorry....*stuff* than they know what to do with, so I'm certain there are tons of things that you could sell and never notice their absence.

This may very well be the only business on the planet that you can start by <u>making</u> money without investing a dime to get started. Besides the obvious, which is immediate cash, your rewards will be numerous. It begins with the most rewarding feeling of empowerment that you could pull off a successful garage sale and put money in your hands to invest back into your business.

Also on the list of benefits is the mental clarity that you gain from de-cluttering your environment...which alone is reason enough to do this. Your mind will be clear and available to work on the next steps. Clutter is a major detriment to success and growth, so we are accomplishing several important things with one little garage sale.

Our objective is to get you started by making some money with the things you already have and then get on to doing more of it, until you are in a business and creating a steady income stream! All the details for making your garage sale a huge success are outlined in the next chapter.

I live in southern California, the land of perpetual sunshine, where garage sales are held year round. However, I grew up in Chicago, where you are lucky if you can get your car out of the garage in the winter and nobody thinks of a garage sale unless it's summer time.

It's a bit trickier, but the weather should not determine our financial success. As you already know, I am a big proponent of "thinking outside the box", and when it comes to your finances, that may be the best advice on the planet. What exactly does this mean in the arena of garage sales? I'm saying that neither snow, nor sleet nor rain, should interfere with your ability to generate money.

In the summer you have lost of competition but having a sale in the winter would make you the only game in town. A few years ago while I was in Chicago around Christmas time, I actually found an estate sale. It was the third day and still busy because there was nowhere else to go. Fortunately, I figured this out a long time ago and my winter sales were absolutely off the charts.

Obviously I'm not suggesting you have a yard sale during a blizzard, but with a little ingenuity you can apply the principles in this book no matter where you live. If you have a basement, that would be a great place to have a sale. Any room in your home that you can block off will work just fine, even the kitchen. All you need is some space to display your things. Consider doing things that most people don't even think of.

The second question people ask me is "Do you sell your things on eBay?" If you've read this far, you know that this book is <u>not</u> about becoming a seller on eBay and it's not what my business is about. I use it, but it's a small part of my business, just one of my resources. It's a great reference place and I certainly have bought and sold many things through this online auction site. I personally like quick action and a quick turn-around and don't care to spend my time on the computer daily, competing with millions of others. I also like to be in control of my prices and auctions are the one place where you could get more than you expected but the opposite is also true and you could be very disappointed.

However, I've made lots of money using it and would certainly recommend you set up an eBay account. It's also a good place to sell rare items because your customer base is the world, instead of just your local area. I once sold a pair of Sevres porcelain candelabras on eBay for $1850. I only paid about $50 for them as part of an estate sale-package deal.

While eBay is a great place to check out going prices, don't let it be your final word. It's helpful in determining values but it's not the definitive be-all and end-all. Especially if you believe you might have something valuable, you have to do your research. Others are checking it out too, so it helps to establish some sort of a starting point of value for any item you have.

One of the biggest challenges with people who use eBay without knowing how it works is that they look at current auctions to see what something is worth and then they quote it as fact. When you use eBay to establish value, don't go to the open auctions, meaning the items that are up for sale right now, rather you want to go to the *sold* category. These are the prices that people have actually paid recently for something. The *selling* price and the *sold* price are two different things entirely.

One of my whimsical friends once listed a photograph that was a cross between a religious apparition and just plain bad photography for one million dollars just for the fun of it. People list all kinds of quirky things for outrageous amounts of money. None of that matters….you need to know what the market place is willing to **pay** for something and that shows up in the "completed listings" category. In order to access this page, you must have an account with a user ID, even if you haven't sold anything.

If you want to master eBay, by all means do so, there are plenty of resources on their website and other sites that have eBay tutorials. I have not spent extensive amounts of time learning all there is to know. I like to have fun and move things quickly and spending countless hours listing things is not fun for me. Let me say however, that while it's too much like *work* as far as I'm concerned, I know many people who make a significant living from their eBay business. I use it only when I think it's the best place to sell what I have.

People imagine that I must have access to some secret directory of resources where I can sell things. They don't believe they can do what I do because they don't have access to this mysterious information. But there truly is no mystery to it…if you only buy things that are extremely well priced you can resell them almost anywhere. However, your buying audience diminishes in direct relation to your prices.

How difficult would it be to profitably resell a gold ring that you bought for $40? Unless you were looking for astronomical profits, I assure you it would not be difficult at all. We apply the same concept to the selling process that we use in the buying process. A good deal at one price is not such a good deal at a higher price. That's true for us and it's true for the people who buy from us. The nature of this business is to get good deals and give good deals.

I learned a long time ago not to hold out for top-dollar. Consequently, I have many dealers who buy from me because there is still room in my prices for them to make a profit. There is so much money out there in the way of stuff/*treasures* that it truly boggles the mind. I like to keep things moving and more importantly, I like to keep the money flowing. That is not to say I give things away dirt cheap, quite the contrary, I'm fair but tend to stick to my prices.

Aside from my unending affection for garage sales, I would encourage you to familiarize yourself with the consignment stores in your area. Each store has its own rhythm and texture and one may turn down something you have, while another would be thrilled to consign the very same item.

It should come as no surprise by now, that the places you buy things are also the best places to sell things. I bought literally hundreds of things from newspaper ads and resold them in the same newspaper just a few days later. I bought things from garage sales and resold them for significant profits at my own garage sales. I have even purchased things in one consignment store and took it to resell in another one. I once bought a large piece of art for $50 in a consignment store, and walked it down the street to my space in an antique mall and sold it for $200 the next day.

Let me clarify that I'm not talking about driving something across town for a $25 dollar profit. I mean high-end items that were not recognized as such, that I bought for a few dollars and sold elsewhere for hundreds and even thousands of dollars. All I did was take a chance on buying something and reselling it elsewhere for a profit....which is all my business is. I once found an old oil painting in a thrift shop for $75 and consigned it in a gallery that sold it for $7500. You just never know what's around the corner...what's behind each door. I had no idea the painting had value, it was just a feeling and a gamble. How did I find the gallery? I went through a few that didn't want it until I got to the one that did. Sometimes it's just a matter of not taking no for an answer.

It becomes an exciting game and you will have lots of fun. I once bought a lovely antique kitchen cupboard in a friend's consignment store, which had been marked down to $75 just to get rid of it and make room for something new. I took it to my store and displayed it in a prominent spot and sold it for $650. Again, the most important aspect of this game is to never over-pay for anything. It makes no difference what the item is as long as you make a profit. While some things have a broader appeal and are easier to sell, there truly are buyers out there for anything and everything.

A friend's son recently shared a great treasure story with me. His company was getting rid of a huge drill press that he was able to buy for $20. He turned around and sold it for $1200. Well done! The rest of the story is that his company sent out over 200 emails to all the employees asking for best offers. You can imagine how many people jumped on that deal, if he won by offering $20. Unfortunately, or perhaps fortunately for the rest of us, most people just don't seem to have an entrepreneurial mindset.

I once bought a metal spiral staircase that was still attached to the outside of a house. Everyone thought I was out of my mind, but I made $500 dollars without lifting a finger. No, I was not about to take it apart and cart it away, it was more of a speculative purchase.

The home owners were remodeling and enthusiastically accepted my hundred dollar offer since they had no idea what to do with it. I'm sure they would have happily given it to me free, just to get rid of it, but I was buying other things and the hundred seemed like the right offer. I put it on eBay for local pick-up-only and sold it for $600 two days later.

I never even met the buyer. He had a truck and tools and he and his friends took it all apart and hauled it away. For a hundred dollars, I took a gamble that paid off. I could have sold it to a scrap-metal dealer and still made money, so it really wasn't much of a gamble. It was a lot of fun because I enjoyed the challenge.

I know that 97% of the population would not have thought of buying that spiral staircase, or may not have had the courage to take the risk. I want you to be among the 3% who would.

I cannot emphasize enough that you have to cultivate a new mind-set before anything else. This business will blossom for you out of that new way of thinking. It's about becoming aware of things around you that you may not have noticed before and seeing for the first time the opportunities that have always been there.

When you to start looking at the world with *"treasure eyes"* you will begin to see the fabulous treasures that are all around you.

Just last week I was shopping in a local consignment store with a girlfriend and found a ladies' gold watch for $250. Its 14k gold and more importantly, the band is also 14k gold and it was clearly marked as such. It doesn't take a genius to figure out that $250 for a gold watch is a great deal, particularly because the band itself is like buying a solid gold bracelet. It's not even about the watch, although it's a well-known name that has a fairly high resale value. If it just sells for scrap, meaning only the value of the gold, there is still far more gold in it than the $250. This is the part where people always get tripped up like my girlfriend who said, "There's no way that can be gold, they would know if it was and wouldn't sell it so cheap." Yes, it is…. and yes, they would…. and yes, they did!

After that it's easy…find the person who will pay you more than the others. Go to jewelers, ask dealers and search out people and places that buy or sell what you have. With gold and other precious metals there is a going rate per ounce. Call and ask what the current price of gold is and if you bought it right, you will make a profit. I would never, ever send gold to some unknown company that advertises on TV or the internet offering to buy your gold and send you cash. Only a negligent and lazy seller would do that.

RECYCLED ELEGANCE

When you sell to a dealer, unless it's a spectacular piece, he is only paying you for the gold. If you want to get better than dealer prices, you have to sell it yourself. Selling a piece of jewelry to someone who wants it for its beauty and style...that's an entirely different value system. A dealer may offer $60 for a ring that you can sell at your upscale garage sale for $260. Always sell to an end user before selling to a dealer.

There are brick and mortar, as well as online stores selling everything from antique buttons to zebra-skin rugs and everything in between. When you have something to sell, it will require a little bit of research on your part. It would take volumes of books and ridiculous amounts of work to compile a halfway decent list that would be obsolete by the time you were reading it. The internet has made research and information gathering very easy and that makes this business easier and faster than ever.

If you believe you have something special, or of great value, there are representatives of the major auction houses like Christie's and Sotheby's in most large cities. They will tell you without cost if your item has the value that would make it worthy of their auctions. These days it takes very little work to take a picture and email it across the country or across the world to get some conversation going about any item you have. It's very helpful to have a good digital camera so you can email pictures to various sources and save yourself much running-around time. (You may start being a savvy non-retail shopper by finding that great digital camera on eBay or through the classifieds...paying pennies on the dollar.) I simply use my phone because it takes excellent, clear pictures.

When it comes to auctions for reselling, you have to be careful. There are many local auction houses and they will be happy to include your items in their next auction, if it's compatible with the nature of their merchandise. Meaning, don't expect an antique action to take on your big-screen TV. However, once the item is in their hands, you have no control how much it sells for. It could go either way...much higher than you expected, but also much lower than you wanted.

Some auction houses will put a *reserve*, which is the price where the bidding starts and if there is no interest, they return your item. Some places are not willing to put reserves so it just sells for whatever amount. There is also the fee they charge, which can be significant, so, if there are very few bidders you can end up losing money. I once took 20 boxes of books to a local auction and got a check for $19. I didn't care because I was inundated and had to make some space, but if I had taken the time and effort to do something else, I would surely have gotten more than one dollar per box, especially since many of them were old. The truth is that I was being a negligent seller. Auctions have an endless variety and sometimes the prices can be ridiculously low, but when it comes to selling I prefer to have more control over my prices.

If you run across vintage clothing, there are many boutiques specializing in exactly that. It's very easy to spot a vintage piece by simply looking at the label. Anyone should be able to distinguish an old label from 50 years ago and something that is newly made. If you look at the quality of the fabric, the workmanship and the style, that too, will be an immediate clue. Some vintage items are very desirable and selling for serious prices. Many celebrities wear vintage gowns not only because they are timeless and beautiful but also by their very nature they are one of a kind and nobody else is likely to be wearing one just like it.

There was a recent story in a local paper about a man who bought a shirt at a garage sale for $5 that turned out to have been owned by Frank Sinatra. The shirt had a date on it as well as the singer's name and the maker and through some research in the library he found pictures of it being worn on stage by Sinatra. You can bet he will make many thousands on his $5 garage sale find.

What exactly is *"vintage"* as it applies to clothes? Basically it's clothing from *"another era"*. In broad terms it's clothing that was made roughly between 1920's up to about 1980. Anything prior to the 1920's would more likely to be considered antique, great for collecting but too delicate to wear. The term *"retro"* applies to the funky clothing from the 1960's and 1970's.

There is no clear-cut definition since it's an ever-evolving genre of clothing more or less defined by the people who are passionate about it. It is tremendous fun if you like fashion and certainly lots of money can be made in the vintage market. One of my friends bought a white Marilyn Monroe style halter dress for a dollar at a garage sale and through a vintage consignment store she got $800 for it.

I once bought some beautiful vintage pieces at an auction in Los Angeles that belonged to Joan Crawford, the movie star. I paid much more than garage sale prices, but I was buying them for myself at the time. Even with the $300 price I paid for one dress that I wore it to a Beverly Hills party, I made a $1000 profit after selling it.

Vintage jewelry is another hot market and I mentioned elsewhere about the man who bought a vintage brooch for $14 and discovered that it's worth over $500,000. Now that's a happy treasure hunting day!

Just as there is no one specific place to look for treasures, there is no one specific place to sell them. They are simply everywhere and can be resold anywhere. When I moved into my new house and went across the street to meet my neighbors they treated me as though I had been sent to save them. As soon as I told them what I do, they had to show me all the stuff they wanted to get rid of. Conversely, if I tell someone that I deal in antique and vintage jewelry, they immediately want to see what goodies I have.

Look for items that have a *unique* look. I bought a coat last year at a garage sale for $1 that looks like a million. It's a denim fabric, but the design and the length and the beautiful flamboyant decorations on it are simply spectacular. I get compliments on it every time I wear it, meaning strangers come up to me and gush over it endlessly. It looked a little weird and wild when I found it on a wire hanger at the garage sale, but you have to train yourself to look for things that are different. On closer inspection, I saw that it was an amazingly cool piece and was quite stunned that they were only asking a dollar for it. The key words are *unique* and *different*. That's what you are looking for. Clothes from the Gap may be functional but its *disposable clothing* and has very little resale value.

When it comes to jewelry, especially for those of us that love the stuff, there is a lot of fun and lots of money to be made. Start by looking for names. The good jewelry of yesteryear has names like: Weiss, Coro, Eisenberg, Dior, Kramer, Kenneth Lane, Schiaparelli, Haskell, and there are many more. The better pieces were signed, (company name stamp) but if something is unique and beautiful people will want it even without a signature. Have a jeweler's loupe with you and take a close look at what you are buying.

The exception is that when you find beautiful old jewelry selling for just a dollar or two please don't whip out your magnifying glass looking for a stamp. Under those circumstances you buy now and look later. Just go by the general look of unique and interesting or beautiful and elegant and buy the stuff. It doesn't take much experience to distinguish the good quality jewelry from the cheap stuff and this is one area where a little education would be useful.

The clasp is always a good indication of quality. The better the piece, the more elaborate the clasp. Also the better pieces are recognizable because of the workmanship. They have a look and feel that is smoother and richer and more sophisticated. There are many details to help you identify better quality jewelry. Semi-precious stones are cold to the touch while artificial ones are not. A genuine pearl is rough when you rub it against your teeth, while a fake one is smooth. The material that costume jewelry is made of is also an indicator of quality and therefore value. The junky pieces seem to be very light and thin while the good stuff has more substance and weight. With just a little attention and comparison you can master this easily. Don't spend too much of your money until you know what you're doing. You can always turn to the internet for ongoing research, but even better would be to visit the high-end swap meets, or vintage stores, where the good stuff is kept in jewelry cases, and get a feel for quality and prices.

Jewelry is the foundation of profitable garage sales and I pointed out in another chapter that you need to build up a fabulous inventory, but do so without spending a big chunk of money. When you see good jewelry and its cheap enough...buy it! Many people are attracted to jewelry, that's why you want to have lots of it available at your sales and that's also why I shop every garage sale by checking out the jewelry before looking at anything else.

I recently helped a friend with a sale and took some of my jewelry along. I had a vintage bracelet that I bought just the day before at a garage sale for $3. It wasn't signed, but it was large and interesting with unique stones and I sold it immediately for $85. That's a nice sweet and easy deal and the lady who got it was thrilled. I could have waited to sell it for $125 but a profit of $82 felt sufficient. It all adds up and at the end of the day we like going home with lots of money.

I like to keep shopping and I like to keep the stuff moving. I made $1400 just from jewelry and we did over $5000 total from her sale in two days from the patio and front lawn only. Nobody went in the house, no big pieces, just boxes of miscellaneous stuff that she wanted to clear out of her storage.

If you are paying to keep things in storage, you're depleting your money for no good reason. The flip side of this story is a perfect illustration of why long term storage is a bad idea. By the time she decided to get rid of the stuff, my girlfriend had spent a ridiculous $3500 on storing it all for a few years. She was lucky to break even and only did so because of my expertise and because she was willing to follow my advice without question. Most people lose several times over with long-term storage.

I never met anyone who felt good about paying for on-going storage. It's a case of holding on to things that are not good enough to take home, but too good to get rid of. You end up paying for your own stuff over and over again in case they should one day become valuable enough to go home with you. It rarely happens therefore storage becomes a tremendous waste of money not to mention a source of guilt. Now that you know how to buy furniture and everything else for pennies on the dollar, you can let go of the old stuff in storage, knowing you can find newer and better things when you're ready for them.

CHAPTER 8

YOU TOO CAN MAKE $4,657 AT YOUR GARAGE SALE

After more than 30 years of being in this exciting business, in case I haven't said it enough: I LOVE GARAGE SALES and I try not to miss too many of them. Whether I'm shopping or having my own, I can't think of a better way to spend a weekend morning. You may not be quite as enthusiastic yet, but when you get into the groove and start making money you'll see why garage sales are the greatest source of endless treasures. Whether you're buying or selling, you'll soon see why garage sales are the best of both worlds.

I once bought a piece of Weller pottery for $10 and sold it to a dealer the same day for $420. How did I know it was Weller? I turned it upside down and read the name on the bottom. I didn't know its value until I did some research online, but I was sure that $10 was a no-brainer deal. I once bought a purse for a dollar that had $300 dollars in it. In fact, as I mention elsewhere, I bought lots of purses with money inside. And found lots of clothes with cash in the pockets and even half-full piggy-banks that nobody bothered to empty.

Over the years, I bought more designer and vintage and couture clothing than I can even begin to recall with substantial resale values. The amount of jewelry I found throughout the years for even less than pennies on the dollar is almost unbelievable.

RECYCLED ELEGANCE

I once bought a heavy gold chain for $1 and my uncle refused to believe that anyone would sell gold for a dollar let alone that it would still be sitting at a moving sale in plain sight at 2:00 in the afternoon.

I suspected that it might be gold, but I was far from certain. I only knew that for $1 it was going home with me. There were no markings that I could see, so we stopped at a jeweler on the way home and asked how much he would be willing to pay for it. After testing that it was gold (which was free) he offered me $275 on the spot. This was before gold went through the roof, but even so I chose to hold on to it and sold it later for $600.

It doesn't matter that at least a hundred people had been through the house and most everything else was gone, the necklace was hanging on a wire coat hanger with a few cheap costume necklaces and nobody paid attention to it. More importantly, like my uncle, everyone immediately discarded the possibility that it might be gold. Don't fall into this trap...meaning don't assume that people know what they are doing and nobody would sell gold for a dollar. I'll say again: I bought incredible amounts of gold and silver over the years for give-away prices.

The majority of people simply don't think this way. I picked up a charming little French country dining room set at a garage sale once for $150 and sold it for $750 in a flash. I bought a fantastic alabaster bust for $150 and sold it to friends with an antique store for $1200. They turned around and sold it to an out of town decorator for $2000. He might have resold it for thousands...who knows? We all made money; however, I took the smallest risk and had the biggest return on my investment.

As with everything else...practice makes perfect. I can't even begin to count how many sales I've done, but certainly enough to know how to make them successful. Once during a sale for a client, one of the neighbors came over wanting to know what I was doing to have 50 people waiting in line long before we opened, since she didn't have that many during her entire two day sale just two weeks earlier. It's really not rocket science, but I do have some good techniques that I learned along the way.

These little how-to secrets are the difference between hundred dollar garage sales and thousand dollar garage sales, consistently. When you get good at it and build up the kind of inventory that I teach, your garage sales should make over a thousand dollars each and every time. It certainly pays to do it right.

The inventory that I'm referring to is jewelry. It's the one thing that's easily portable, commands the highest prices, and grabs most people's attention. The way to start building jewelry inventory is to start buying the stuff in bulk. Where to start? Garage sales, of course!

Almost every garage sale has a bunch of jewelry thrown about for just a few dollars per piece. The perception of value, or rather the *lack* of value comes from the fact that people just toss it all in a box and buyers are free to sort through it. You can just grab the whole box and ask how much they want for it. You would be surprised how little people ask when you buy a whole batch of something. I saw a woman scoop up about 30 CD's once that were marked $1 each and without thinking it through, the sellers accepted her $5 offer!

When you buy the whole lot, you will most likely end up with a mix...meaning some great stuff and some not so great stuff. A couple of the better pieces should get back your investment when you sell them...which makes all the other pieces you subsequently sell, pure profit. What you don't want to do is buy a ring for $5 and wait to resell it for $10. You cannot afford to have $5 tied up in inventory that may not sell for a while and doubling your money is simply not enough. You want to buy these things for just pennies and have a huge variety to include in your sales.

I once spent $2000 on an incredible collection of jewelry that included everything from jade to diamonds. There were so many pieces that I finally gave up trying to inventory all of it. Two thousand dollars sounds like a huge gamble, but I sold just one necklace from that collection for $6500. It was made by a famous Greek jeweler whose clients included Onassis and the name was stamped on the clasp. It was a stunning necklace with diamonds and even the untrained eye would have seen that it was unique and valuable. I sold the matching earrings separately for $1200. I had recovered my investment AND had a $5700 profit, before I sold another piece. That means that not only did I pocket $5700 but everything else from that moment on was 100% profit.

I suddenly had a huge inventory and everything I sold from that point on would be free money. That's why you never put $5 into some $10 or even a $20 trinket. Think big, big, big and save your money for the **big** deals. If you keep playing the game, which means keep looking, you will find big deals and jewelry is one of the best places to invest your money. Gold and silver will never lose their value and will certainly keep going up and since you are buying all of it way below market value anyway, for you it goes up just between buying it and re-selling it. That's something you can count on. Even if the necklace along with the earrings sold for only $2000, the rest of my inventory would still have been free, so it was not a big gamble.

When selling jewelry, you have to do what the jewelers do; meaning display your pieces in the most attractive manner possible. That means investing in glass cases that not only show off what you have, but more importantly protect your valuables.

At times you may have ten people standing around wanting to see something in your cases, but it's very easy to get confused, so make sure to give out no more one or two of the valuable pieces at a time and close the case until those pieces have been returned. This is not-negotiable and customers are not allowed to leave your sight while they have your jewelry in their possession. Don't let anyone pressure you...it's better to let buyers wait than to have something valuable disappear. And trust me: things will disappear if you're not ultra-careful! This applies especially to the gold pieces, and anyone who works my jewelry table knows that I am extremely strict about this rule. It also creates more excitement and a higher demand for your items when people have to push about in a crowd just to get to the good stuff.

Now that you are working on your inventory, we can move on to the details that will make your sales super successful. Let's start with the most important part; which is getting people to come to your sale. You can have the most fantastic merchandise, but it won't do you much good if nobody knows about it. So, our number one objective is to get the maximum amount of people to show up at our sales.

Even in a high traffic area, hanging a sign at the corner is not enough. You can set up in the middle of Times Square and not get the results you want because the people who are passing by are either too busy to stop, or don't care about sales, or would rather die than stop at a garage sale, or don't have cash with them, or intend to stop back later, (but forget) or can't afford to buy anything, or didn't see you, etc.

Our first objective is to attract the crowd of habitual garage sale shoppers. These people look in the paper searching for bargains and deals and they literally make a habit of going to garage sales on a regular basis. They are already out there...all you have to do is get their attention and make sure they come to your sale before spending all their money elsewhere.

Some of them are dealers, for others it's a passion or a hobby or an addiction, but the fact is that there is a huge crowd in any good area that follows the garage sale circuit on weekends. These people are pre-qualified, because they know how things work and even more importantly, they come with cash! They are reliable buyers who show up repeatedly because they read the ads before determining where to go. That's why a successful garage sale starts with an ad that sizzles.

YOU TOO CAN MAKE $4,657 AT YOUR GARAGE SALE

Your potential buyers have read hundreds of ads and they know what words to look for. Not long ago, classified newspaper ads were the place to go, but, the internet has changed the world of newspapers in a big way and now most people turn to **Craigslist**...and it's free.

Let's look at what turns people on and off when reading ads. For starters; no garage sale aficionado wants to go to a sale that advertises baby clothes, toys, or anything child related. That's a completely different customer. The mentality behind this is that people who have kids spend their disposable income on their kids and most likely won't have anything worthwhile to sell. This may or may not be true (but it most often is) and I didn't make it up, it's simply how people think. Advertisers spend millions to understand how their customers think and you have to do the same.

People gloss over small average ads and get hooked by the bigger ones with substance. There are also keywords that buyers look for when reading ads. Check out these two ads. Which one excites you more?

<u>**Garage Sale**</u> Furniture, clothing, shoes, toys, books, tools, art, lots of misc.

OR:

<u>**Garage Sale**</u> 30 years accumulation must be sold this weekend! Treasures from all over the world, including tons of gold and vintage jewelry, interesting antiques, fabulous designer and vintage clothing, shoes and purses, 50's furniture, garage full of tools,

large art collection, electronics, huge amount of miscellaneous. All must go at give-away prices!!

As you can see, the first ad is boring and not likely to motivate anyone to rush right over. There is nothing about it that creates excitement or a sense of urgency to get there. People respond to words by creating pictures in their head and the second ad sounds alluring because it paints a picture of exciting, wonderful, hidden treasures and opens the mind to dreams of finding fabulous deals among all the goodies.

You want your ad to be irresistible, like an infomercial with such a compelling message that people reach for the phone in the middle of the night. It's not the product; it's the presentation that is compelling. Does anybody really need a rotisserie oven, a food dehydrator or a counter-top grill? Those companies have made millions by painting very compelling pictures of how their particular product will make life better.

This is exactly what we want our ads to do. If there are 20 other garage sales in the paper, you want your ad to stand out from the others, thereby diverting the people who are already going to the sales, to come to yours....and come yours first!

Never, ever put your phone number in your ads unless your sale is by appointment only. You don't want people calling day and night wanting to beat out the crowd, or asking questions to determine if you have anything they want.

Sometimes the very ambitious (or aggressive) will knock on your door the day before with some line so you let them in to look, also trying to beat out all the others. This is not something you want to allow. Letting people in early to cherry pick you best stuff will diminish your success in more ways than one. Don't let anyone persuade you into falling for this. Sorry...they just have to show up at the sale like everyone else.

It goes without saying that your ads should be truthful. Don't advertise "tons of jewelry" if you only have a few trinkets or claim to have things that you don't have. It's important to establish credibility, that's what you are building your business on. The number one attractor seems to be jewelry. Other things that attract customers are words like, designer, antique, vintage, collectible, electronics, paintings, mid-century-modern, art deco, art nouveau, leather, furniture, tools, .

While our first objective is to attract the regular garage sale crowd, our second objective is to attract everyone else. This falls under the category of anyone who is in town and... breathing. The best way to accomplish this is by going to the places where people go and let them know about your event. This would include posting fliers in high-traffic areas like the supermarket, or health-food store, church or other places where people gather and even at the swap meet. You can make up fliers and put them on cars and ask your friends to give them out to their circle. If you are super ambitious, you can deliver them to the homes in your neighborhood or see if your kid's school would be willing to let you post some of them.

You might consider different start times on different ads. If you said 8am in the paper, 9am would be better on the fliers. Being very busy is good, being mobbed...not so much.

You may want to ask some girlfriends to bring some friends by for coffee and doughnuts. If you tell them that they can bring just a few things that you'll sell for them, they will be more motivated to do so. I would limit the number of items they can drop off; otherwise you will be overwhelmed keeping tabs on people's stuff. It would be even better to ask your friends to come and help with the sale.

I have to admit that I've never bothered to do the fliers or any other personal promotions for any of my sales. It isn't mandatory, but it's an option, should you be super ambitious. I have an email list of people who signed up to be notified when I have sales and sometimes I'm even too busy to notify those people. This is admittedly negligent on my part, but proof that it's the advertising that pulls in the crowd. However, as I said: posting your ad on Craigslist is an absolute *must*...at least the day before.

If you did a good job with your ads and the weather is good, you should have a great turnout. What's a great turnout? My sales always have people waiting in line before we open. Even the ones I've done for the fifth time in the same location, the turnout is very good. You will need the most help when you first open, because that's when the majority of buyers show up and it can be total chaos.

You can do a sale together with some friends or ask your neighbors if they want to participate. Make sure that everyone does something to promote the event. If you treat it as an important event, others will catch your mood and do the same. In this case your ad should read *multi-family* sale or *neighborhood sale,* always remembering to use the keywords that attract.

Something else you might try and I have made lots and lots of money doing this...have your sale one place on Friday and somewhere else on Saturday. You will have a much bigger turnout if they are fresh sales on both days than you would by running one sale for two days in the same location.

The next important part of attracting buyers is to put up lots of good signs. Signs should absolutely, positively be posted by the night before. There are too many things to do the morning of the sale, and people show up very early, you can't be running around last minute worrying about signs.

Signs that bring buyers have the following details: they're big and bright to capture attention from far away, have a big, bold arrow pointing the way, they're posted where easy to see, have only the necessary information: type of sale, date and time and address, are sturdy and properly secured and have large letters that are easy to read from a distance.

You will need a hammer and nails, clear strong packing tape and rope to get your signs properly posted. I like to hang them very high, where it's easily visible for drivers and won't be blocked by cars. I like thick, colored paper, because it catches attention. Make sure it's attached properly. You will lose customers if the wind has blown down half of the sign and people have to get out of the car to read what's on it.

The reason for the big bold arrow is to make it easy for drivers to turn, even at the last minute. Once people pass a sign they may just keep going, but if you make it easy for them, it's like leaving breadcrumbs...they will follow. I use very big markers and write on both sides of the sign and draw a huge arrow across the bottom. When you put it up, either side will work because the arrows are pointing in the right direction and if you do repeat sales you can re-use the signs.

Now that we have handled the most important aspects of how to get the maximum amount of people to your sale, let's go on to how to have a wildly successful sale. The title of this chapter is "You Too Can Make $4,657 at YOUR Garage Sale", because I've done exactly that, and want you to do the same. Does that happen every time? No, but my sales are never under $1000 and very often well over $2000. I'm talking about garage sales, NOT moving sales or estate sales.

There are plenty of garage sale shoppers with cash and they are eager to spend, but you must have good merchandise at good prices. Obviously the final tally depends on the inventory; even the best ad can't generate money if there is nothing for people to buy.

Moving sales and estate sales attract the same people and a lot more of them and it's quite possible to make ten and well over twenty thousand dollars on a weekend, depending of course, on the contents of the house. It's the same process as a garage sale, with obviously lots more high-ticket items.

You also want to create a desire for your items, so everything must be displayed properly and attractively so they can be seen and wanted. For starters, everything should be clean. If you don't want to deal with cleaning certain things, that's OK, but you will have to discount it accordingly. It's also a good idea to group things together; you don't want to be hiding the cordless drill among the lingerie.

You will have to make an investment in some tables, as they will be necessary for all your sales. I also prefer to use tablecloths, especially for the better quality merchandise. Anything that has a solid color will do, but my preference is a heavier drapery fabric that looks rich and hangs very long, so I can hide bags and boxes under the tables.

Tablecloths look attractive and they represent a seller with good taste, which to the buyer means good quality merchandise. This may be on an unconscious level, but trust me that everything counts. You can use sheets for starters, but there are plenty of tablecloths or drapes you can buy at garage sales for just a few dollars.

Set up your tables so people can easily maneuver between them. I like to place my tables so that buyers are on one side and I am on the other, but you can experiment with what feels right to you.

I prefer using masking tape over stickers for labeling and pricing. It doesn't leave a sticky mess when you remove it, but also doesn't come off until you take it off. You can use a thick colored marker to write on it and cut (or tear) off as large a size as needed. Bundle it around sheets sets, or napkin sets, anything you want to keep intact, and write clearly what's in the bundle so people won't have to rip it apart to see what's there. This alone will make your life much easier. There are little round price stickers you can buy that are pre-priced and very easy to use. Be careful, however, because people have been known to switch tags.

At my sales I don't have boxes hiding under tables and everything is fully visible to buyers. The things that are in boxes are books and they are all facing the same direction so it's easy to read the titles. I try to think of what I like when I'm shopping and implement those things for my customers. Two things you must have are bags and plenty of change. The idea is to make it easy and pleasant to do business with you. Have lots singles, tens and five dollar bills, because people will show up with large bills and if you can't make change things become stressful.

In California it's customary to throw a sheet on the ground and throw clothes on it, but this implies lack of value and you won't command high prices that way. To get top prices, clothes should be on hangers and on a clothing rack, neat and organized. If you have a large mirror, hang it somewhere so your buyers can make easier decisions. Sometimes people will ask to use your house to try things on, but that's a definite no-no...allowing strangers in your house is never a good idea and neither is getting distracted from your sale.

Always keep an eye on your valuable merchandise. My jewelry is always in glass cases and the valuable items are in front of me. Even if the jewelry is not gold it's under glass. It creates a perception of higher value than tangled up trinkets sitting on the table. It's not only for easy display but I don't want anyone walking off with my stuff. It may be a fact of life that some people feel OK with taking things that belong to others, but let's not encourage bad behavior by our negligence.

I have been to moving sales where people left their wallets on the bedroom dresser, their jewelry in plain sight or their purse or money lying around while strangers were walking through the house. That's absolutely nuts...how much effort does it require to put your things in a secure place?

Be sure to block off the areas where no one is allowed with tape or a chair, whatever it takes to keep people out. If you're not selling the contents in the closet or the cabinets...make sure to tape it off and put a sign, otherwise every single cabinet and drawer and closet will be opened...the hidden stuff is always more desirable.

In an indoor sale, otherwise known as a *house sale,* the rules are that everything in every room is for sale unless otherwise indicated. The large items that you are keeping can stay right where they are but need to be clearly marked with a big **sold** sign. The small items have to be packed away. If an item gets sold during the sale, you also put a sold sign on it.

Speaking of items being sold, when do you collect payment on larger items? The cleanest deals are the ones where you are paid immediately. You then give the buyer a time frame that is acceptable to both of you in which they have to get their merchandise out.

When you get into deposits and holding things without money, it can get messy. The reason for the sale in the first place is to sell as much as possible during this limited window of opportunity. That means you can't hold things for people without a deposit while they go jogging or to breakfast, etc. *Everything is for sale until someone pays for it.*

Never take small deposits on high priced items. You can't agree to hold a $300 sofa with a $20 deposit. That won't do because if the deposit is too small, people can easily change their mind and walk away from the deal, since they don't have any real money invested. You, on the other hand, will be stuck with the sofa and chasing after someone who has no intention of coming back. Make sure to let the buyer know that the deposit is not-refundable, and if you give a receipt, write it on there as well. The $300 dollar sofa must have a minimum of a $100 deposit and while you're at it, take names and numbers from other people who are interested...just in case. Don't put **sold** on anything until it's paid.

In the process of displaying your goods, I seriously recommend that you price everything in advance with easy to read stickers. It makes things infinitely easier and you won't be running in 12 different directions, frantically trying to come up with last minute sensible prices. I don't always follow this rule, but I have done so many sales that if someone woke me up from a deep sleep and set me down in the midst of a hectic sale, I could come up with prices on the spot.

Many of the rules in the chapter on *How to Shop Garage Sales* applies here...be sure to go back and re-read it. First rule is not to allow anyone to distract you. During a busy sale you need to keep your wits about you and stay very focused. Dressing right with appropriate pockets and plenty of change is vital. Also make sure you don't need to run in the house for things during busy times and always make sure the door to the house is secured. I did a sale with a girlfriend in one of L.A.'s best areas that drove this point home so I could share it with you.

In the middle of a very hectic sale right in front of everyone, I looked up and saw a guy sneaking into the house. It was clear that nothing inside was part the sale, since everything was displayed on the patio and the lawn. The front door was closed and he had to walk up three steps to even get to it. I ran and yanked him back, none too gently, just as he was half-way through the door! If I hadn't seen him just in that second, he would have been inside doing who-knows-what and probably escaping through the back. Earlier, we had been looking through the beautiful jewelry she had inherited, so there was thousands of dollars' worth of valuable that he most likely would have found. My high-strung girlfriend immediately grasped the disaster that had just been averted and she let him have it while he went scampering off with his tail between his legs. It's a delicate area because someone can always claim they made a mistake and you can't wrestle them to the ground and search them. It's much easier to keep the door locked….seriously!

Pricing is an art in and of itself. You want to be high enough, without being overpriced. I don't want any of my readers selling gold jewelry, or cashmere sweaters for fifty cents. This is another reason you need a computer. You don't want to sell things for pennies without doing the proper research. This is a must and it takes almost no time to type something into a search engine before pricing it.

Unfortunately, I can't give you a formula for garage sale pricing because there isn't one. Some items command a higher price simply because more people want it. You might get more for a sought-after book that just came out, than you would for a $150 pair of shoes. If you have uncertainly in this area, it would be a good idea to take yourself to several garage sales before having your own, just to get a feel for what's going on. If people are running off with the stuff like it's free, it's probably underpriced, but if lots of things are still sitting there and it's past noon, prices are probably too high. Don't worry about this, you will begin to get a feel for things, and your pricing will work itself out soon enough.

That's why it's vital to your business to only buy things at very good prices, because when it comes time to sell, even if you discount some of your things, you still make a profit. And if there were some undervalued treasures in your previous purchases, now you can sell them for a more serious dollar amount.

If you plan to do lots of garage sales, you will have to find different locations to hold them. After people have been to a few of your sales at the same address, the excitement factor and therefore, the number of buyers will diminish. Make arrangements with friends to have sales together with them at their homes. Make it attractive for them, by offering to take care of the ad and even help them organize and sell their things. I have done this with lots of friends and now they chase me to have sales because we have great fun and we make money, while clearing out stuff that's become clutter.

You can also approach someone who lives in a high traffic area to let you use their driveway or lawn and offer to pay them or offer to sell some of their items in exchange.

This book is very much about *community*, which in my opinion is the place to spend our money and also the place to put our collective energies. There are many creative ways to get people together and support each other to turn unwanted things into cash.

This is a beautiful business in every way and while you are creating a very lucrative income stream, you can help others to do the same. A block sale is probably the most fun of all. The women have fun spending time together and organizing and on sale day the whole neighborhood is out having a grand old time! It conjures up images of life in the 50's, where the kids have lemonade stands and people are talking and connecting and enjoying a beautiful sunny day. Again, it's the community spirit. Knowing our neighbors and feeling connected is incredibly valuable. It's good to know that our neighbors will look out for our kids if need be and they will, if we make an effort to get to know them.

Now that you are learning to buy great things at great prices and learning how to successfully re-sell them, you have to keep the flow going. Make sure you have purge-sales periodically and clear out the things that are not generating interest. If you reduced the prices and the stuff is still not leaving, you should consider donating it. It is counterproductive to get bogged-down with too much stuff... it creates overwhelm.

I have given away enormous amounts of stuff through the years; sometimes it was a matter of saving my sanity, especially when I had stores and things would be coming in the front door faster that we could process it all. Purging old stuff and old energy is healthy and cleansing. When you buy things by the roomful, much of it is free and you can afford to pass it on to someone else. Moving boxes of junk from one place to another is not progress.

Once you get good at doing sales, you might consider turning that talent into a business. It was never my intention to get hired by someone to hold their sale, but why not? Years ago when people started asking me to do their sales it dawned on me that I had a valuable skill. Estate sale people have been around for a long time, but doing moving sales and even garage sales for others is kind of a new idea you might want to consider.

I pick and choose the sales I do with the stipulation that I bring my jewelry and whatever else I want, to any sale that I do. The sellers are never allowed at the sale, we have that agreement up front...that's why they hired me. That would be like doing your homework with the teacher looking over your shoulder...not very comfortable. If they want to be part of the sale and do part of the work, I still get the same commission and put them to work as I would any other employee. I have yet to meet a seller that wanted to do that. They are happy to stay far away.

My commission generally ranges between 30 and 50 percent... closer to 30% if there are many large ticket items. Those are obviously a lot less work, since all you have to do is stick a price tag on. If there's an endless amount of small things that need to be processed or furniture that's not the greatest, I prefer not to do it for less than 50%.

If doing this as a business appeals to you and you have children, you could put everyone to work and even pay them a small percentage. What a great little family business! The kids could research things on the internet, help you move things around, get things priced, cleaned and organized while learning the business. You would be giving your children two of the greatest gifts: *self-reliance* and the ability to *manage money,* while addressing the two major complaints in America today: Not enough money and not enough time with family. It's genius!

CHAPTER 9

PENNIES ON THE DOLLAR DECORATING

I have a house full of beautiful and unique furnishings and décor accent pieces, yet I rarely step foot into a retail store. As I look around my living room, I see a pair of antique leather chairs that I bought for $125 each. I love those chairs and consider them *keepers*. That may change in the future, but it's nice to know that I don't have to sell any of my things at a loss; rather I can sell ALL of them for a profit. There is an exquisite floor lamp that's designed with ram's heads in a very intricate metal carving that I bought for $25. I bought another floor lamp, hand-carved solid dark wood for a mere $5. The shade on it is very cool and unique, a painted bamboo, which was also $5 at a garage sale while visiting friends in Las Vegas.

I have a Maitland-Smith candle holder with the $295 price tag still on the bottom that I acquired for pennies as part of a large purchase. On my wall is a light fixture that I saw for $450 in one of the local high-end stores but I bought for $75 at a sale. (I may have paid too much for that one, but I bought it for myself) I have an oil painting from a well-known local artist which would sell in her gallery for $400 which I bought for $10. The gold frame is worth over $100! I have another wonderful little oil painting also from a prominent local artist that was also $10.

I have a bronze figurine worth a couple of thousand dollars that I bought for $200 at an auction several years ago and another bronze on my sofa table that came out of an incredible estate. I love my two goddess hand-carved Asian statues. They are unique and lovely and very elegant at 42" tall. I bought them for the ridiculously low price of $25 from someone who lived and worked in Asia for a few years. Little did he know when he hand-carried them back to the U.S. that he was bringing them back for me.

The lamp on my coffee table is from a well-known interior design firm that was going out of business after 30 years. It had a crazy $1200 price tag on it but I bought a number of things and they wanted to wrap it up already, so I got it for $100. It's unique and substantial, all hand-painted and the shade alone is well worth the price.

You can always tell a good quality lamp by the shade. Another way to distinguish a good quality lamp is by the finial. That's the little knob that screws on and holds the shade to the lamp. Good quality finials are desirable and when you see one buy it and hold on to it. I have an interesting collection...never know when I might need one to dress up a lamp.

If you are going to be in this business it's also a good idea to save the harps from lamps, in different sizes and heights. That's the part that attaches to the base of the lamp and holds the shade and finial. If you change out a shade, you may have to change the harp as well to adjust to the height of the new shade.

Something else I buy whenever I see them reasonably priced is seashells. I have a huge collection and I enjoy adding to it for just a few dollars. Last year I found a very large glass lamp for 50 cents that was filled with beautiful seashells. The metal on the lamp had oxidized making it look rusty and unattractive, but I didn't care about that.

When I got home, I unscrewed the bottom plate and removed all the beautiful seashells. Amazing that the sellers hadn't thought of doing the same thing; they could have sold the shells for at least $10 instead of giving the lamp away for 50 cents. Apparently none of the other shoppers had thought of doing this either.

Once in a while I will buy fabric, but only if it's absolutely exquisite...I don't sew personally, and don't want to clutter up my life with things I don't use. If I do find something really fantastic, I have a lady who will sew it for me into whatever I design. It's a lot of fun to create an idea in your head and watch it turn into something you can wear or use for decorating.

Some people would tell you not buy something unless you have an immediate use for it. While I agree with this organizing tip for the most part, if you enjoy decorating and creating a beautiful home environment, it makes sense to buy things for pennies on the dollar that you know you will use sometime in the future.

I would add that you should only do this if you are organized and have the space. I buy broken jewelry pieces for the stones and to decorate clothing, shoes or purses. When the urge strikes me, I like to play with these things and create something new and interesting. For jewelry that needs repair, I have plenty of stones on hand, probably enough for a good sized mosaic, but fortunately they don't require much space and for me it's fun and relaxing to be creative this way.

If this is not your thing, find something that is and buy it when you go to sales. I also buy notebooks and stationary and miscellaneous small tools and I have a ton of pens and markers and highlighters. Some of these pens are famous name-brands worth hundreds of dollars and on the lower end, why pay $8 for just one of the newer pens when you can buy a handful of them for less than a dollar?

The savings will add up and you'll soon realize that the things you used to run out and buy for retail prices are now staples and you no longer have to concern yourself with them. Most people really don't believe me when I say they can buy anything and everything from cleaning products to trash bags to gold rings for a quarter at garage sales….it's wild!

When buying furniture, look for pieces that are well made. Don't waste your money on anything that's inferior quality. The internet has made research so incredibly easy, there is no excuse for buying junk.

My Drexel bamboo dining room set was $500 from a lady who was moving. I also acquired her beautiful Drexel solid wood décor shelf unit. At the time I had no idea what I would do with it, but it was too stunning to pass up for $150, and now I love it too much to part with it. I like an air of timeless elegance, with a little *edgy flair* thrown in and I want things that are elaborate and beautifully made. These never go out of style and always command higher resale prices.

All my candles are from garage sales. I love candles, but why pay retail when I can have drawers full of them for what one or two would cost in a store? How about a 20 inch candle with an $80 price tag on the bottom that only cost $5? I have a beautiful wool rug and I appreciate the fact that it was brand new when I bought it for $20 dollars at a garage sale. I mentioned earlier my two giant flower pots outside that were $20 each at a garage sale. I have two very cool leather pillows from a high-end retailer on my couch that I found also at a garage sale for $2 each.

In my office I have another leather pillow that has a beautiful hand-painted tiger on it and I only paid one dollar for that one. My friends know how I shop, yet they are still amazed at the things I find. Why would someone sell an obviously expensive leather pillow with hand-painted art on it for one dollar? I really don't know, and I don't care. All we need to know is that people sell things for next-to-nothing, and they do so constantly on any given day in every town across the country.

I love beautiful pillows but they are one of the most overpriced things you can buy. It's crazy to pay hundreds of dollars for a decorative pillow! I am very particular and only buy ones that are brand new or in almost new condition. You want to make sure to buy them only from a pet-free and smoke-free home and make sure it smells fresh and clean.

This applies to everything you buy, but in particular any item with fabric. I would never buy a couch that needed to be cleaned or needs spots removed. It reflects sloppy owners and costs too much in time, effort and money to clean. You also run the risk of the spots not coming out, which makes the piece completely worthless.

My fabulous down sofa was custom ordered from the design center for $6000 by someone who never picked it up. It went to a consignment store and that's where I fell in love with it and bought it for $1600. Relatively speaking that's a lot more than I usually pay for things, but it's beautiful and unique and superbly made. Even the feather-down is top quality and best of all I have not seen another sofa like it anywhere. I've had it for several years and still would not part with it. The chenille fabric shows no sign of wear and has not faded one bit even though the California sun shines through the window almost daily. That's why I spent $1600. If you go to a retailer, that same amount of money would buy you a couch that's only worth a few hundred dollars at best.

I avoid as much as possible any furniture that's currently made in China. It's made with inferior quality materials and treated with many different chemicals, which continue to out-gas for a long time. That means you breathe a toxic chemical compound in your own home, every minute of every day. This can become a serious health risk and there is no furniture on the planet worth getting sick over.

I bought a small foot-stool a while back for a dollar at a garage sale to recover with leather when I felt the urge to be creative. I took some leather pieces that I had saved from another sale and spent some time covering the entire footstool with it. I noticed that the leather had a very strong smell that was giving me a headache as I worked on it, but assumed that it would eventually disappear.

I stored my newly completed very attractive creation under my coffee table and forgot about it, but every time I sat on the couch I noticed an unpleasant chemical smell. The chemicals that are used to treat the leather are toxic and I finally had to get rid of my masterpiece.

I went to a parking lot sale a few months later and one of the stores was selling gorgeous leather remnants. They had large boxes outside in the fresh air and the chemical smell was still overwhelming. Now I only buy old leather pieces, like designer skirts or coats made from soft, fine leather, that nobody wants, for a couple of dollars. I grant you that some people are more sensitive than others, but being able to tolerate the toxic chemicals without immediate physical reaction does NOT mean that it's not doing damage to your body. We already live in a world filled with chemicals; we have to find every way possible to lessen the toxic load on ourselves and our children who have delicate immune systems.

This reason alone is serious enough to stay away from newly made retail furniture. Any new item and that includes kitchen cabinets and carpeting; is treated with chemicals and will continue to poison your indoor air whether or not you can smell it. You can protect your health by buying pre-owned furniture. The longer something's been around, the more likely it is that the out-gassing has stopped or at least diminished significantly.

This is an issue that involves the health of your family and it's worth the time to do your own research. Major problems continue to surface with Chinese-made products following episodes in recent years involving contaminated toothpaste and pet-food ingredients, lead-tainted toys and defective tires along with the toxic dry-wall fiasco. I'm sure this is still only the beginning and other serious problems will continue to come to light. It's a problem that you can leave out of your life by not buying things made in China and shopping instead in your community at garage and estate and moving sales. Yes, everything comes back full circle to that central idea.

Another unpleasant aspect of new furniture from China is bugs. There are plenty of horror stories of bed bugs and tiny termites along with beetles and moths that wreak havoc with unsuspecting consumers. I personally had two pieces that were infested with the termites or woodworm. They make tiny holes and you know you have them when you see a small pile of wood-dust that keeps accumulating seemingly out of nowhere. One of these pieces was a new "carved wood" very attractive sink base cabinet with a granite top.

This piece was a consignment in my store and while it was beautiful, it was a challenge from day one. The granite top broke when the movers touched it and had to be repaired. The sink started to crack right down the middle for no apparent reason and eventually had to be repaired. The base had some small bug infestation which left that little telltale dust-mound on the bottom of the inside.

It's only a matter of time before the sink falls through from the bugs eating away at the supporting frame. You also run the risk of these bugs traveling to your other furniture and throughout your house. It's basically a very attractive piece of garbage.

If you are re-doing a bathroom and need a new sink base, here is a better idea: find a chest of drawers or small buffet that you love and have it converted. If you own your own home, your greatest return on your investment will be from upgrading the kitchen and bathrooms. It's worth the additional expense to pay a professional to alter the top two drawers to make room for the plumbing and cut a hole in the top. A custom ordered granite top will be the most expensive part, but it's well worth it for a beautiful one-of-a-kind look that enhances the value of your home. If you choose not to use granite, there are sealers to prevent water from damaging the original wood finish.

I have done this with bathrooms for myself as well as clients and the end result always looks beautiful and elegant. If you select rich colors for your wall, your bathroom will look smashing!

I have a beautiful light fixture in my guest bathroom that was $175 retail, which I got at a garage sale for $2, still in the box with the price tag on it. Look for unique and beautiful things and imagine what they would look like in your house. If you get them home and it doesn't look as good as you expected, you can resell the items for a profit and look for something else. If you should want to re-decorate your home you can sell everything and start all over. This system is so beautiful...you either make money now or you make money later.

I have beautiful silk flowers and I mean the high-end-looks-like-real ones that are all from sales along with my gorgeous silk palm trees. Some of my flowers cost over $20 *per piece* retail and I bought them for pennies. Silk flowers add color and beauty to any room and are well worth buying.

I have an exquisite little Italian antique hall table made of finely detailed metal with a marble top that I only paid $35 for and had an offer to sell for $300.

My brand new leather barstools were only $30 each. On rare occasions when I go browsing in retail furniture stores I am amazed by the price of bar-stools. Why would anyone pay $1,200 for a bar-stool? The mechanisms are similar in all of them, the amount of fabric is minimal yet the prices are outrageous. Nobody buys just one and paying the price of a cruise for three barstools seems crazy.

I am certainly not disputing the fact that there is a vast difference in quality, but it comes off an assembly line and there is simply no reason for it to be so expensive. That same barstool at $300 would still be expensive, but certainly more palatable. My point is that the large corporations are making obscene profits and the consumers are going broke. We have to take our power back and think not just twice, but several times where and how we spend our money.

If you are looking to fill your home with beautiful, great quality furniture and accent pieces, buying from a private party is the only way to go. My first choice would be classified ads from people who are moving. They are motivated and ready to go and you won't believe the deals you'll find.

Once you get a whiff of the sweet smell of bargains, you will want to kick yourself for not doing this sooner. No worries, better late than never, but I can assure you that you won't go back to retail. This is simply too much fun!

I have gorgeous Waterford glasses and a collection of Baccarat crystal along with other exquisite European cut crystal and an interesting collection of vintage martini shakers. I have a selection of fine vintage wines from 1960's and 70's that make spectacular gifts. Some of these wines like Chateau Lafite Rothschild are selling online for over $500! It's a very cool gift...for which I only paid a few dollars.

I have a $4000 Italian leather couch in the den that I bought for $300 and a Ralph Lauren leather ottoman that currently sells in a local high-end furniture store for an unbelievable $2,395! Why would anyone pay that much for an ottoman simply because of a designer tag on the bottom that isn't even visible unless you turn it over?

For that price I want Ralph to personally handcraft it with love just for me and bring it with him when he comes for dinner. I will handle the cooking and the wine, Ralph. The second option would be to buy it from someone else for $150, which is what I did.

A few months ago, a friend was looking for a sofa and I found a leather one for him in perfect condition with recliners at both ends for $100. How exciting to find a three thousand dollar leather couch for the price of dinner!

Here is a great tip for creating a beautiful home environment for pennies on the dollar: **Upgrade as you go along.** Instead of living in an empty place until you find what you want at the prices you can afford, buy something that's very well priced and replace it with something better later.

The same friend who got the couch was looking for something decorative to go in front of his fireplace, but couldn't find anything he liked. In the same house where I found the couch, there was a small attractive hand-painted slender cabinet for a mere $10. One of the knobs had come off, but we found it in a drawer and actually the knobs could easily be replaced to give it a whole new look.

With a little attention it turned out to be a very good-looking little piece and fits perfectly in the small space. It may not have been the definitive piece for my friend but I explained that he could use it until he found exactly what he wanted and he could sell this little cutie at a garage sale for much more than $10. It made great sense and it looks so good in his home that now he doesn't want to part with it.

I have been upgrading for years and hardly any of my furniture is what I owned 10 years ago. That's another reason to buy non- retail. Styles and tastes change and you don't want to hold on to things that you no longer love just because you paid too much for it and now feel obligated to keep it.

One of my girlfriends paid an insane price of $3,600 for just a coffee table that's now out of style. She hates her living room furniture, but her husband refuses to let her go out and spend thousands more for new stuff. No, she did not know me at the time and she would never do that again. If you add the price of the over-priced sofa and two chairs she could have bought a Rolex watch with diamonds instead that she could now be reselling for twenty thousand dollars. Instead she has a living room full of furniture that's no longer desirable and she will be lucky to get a few hundred dollars for all of it.

I paid $100 for my brand new still-in-the-box Noritake china that retails for $700. My sterling flatware came from sales as did my gorgeous linen table cloths. I have a collection of hand-carved elephants from Africa ...not the new ones from China... in my office which is also my *"safari room"*. I have a magnificent picture of a tiger in a frame with triple matting that came from an auction for $150. In the evenings I turn on the light for ambiance and I recently found out that this particular light above the picture, that I only paid a dollar for at a garage sale retails for $150! This is so much fun!

I have an antique Asian cabinet in my office that I use for files and papers which only cost $150. It's a very attractive and interesting piece and I have even used it in the living room as a liquor cabinet in the past. Its fun to find new uses for old pieces of furniture, all it takes is a little imagination.

My home is filled with gorgeous things and almost all of it came from the secondary market. For the same $1800 that I foolishly spent on a vacuum cleaner, I could have furnished a room with tasteful, elegant pieces and still had plenty of money left. You just have to know how to shop and you are learning it right here.

I once purchased Hunter-Douglas blinds with attached sheers for $500. The lady had them in her house less than a month and after paying $2300, she decided she didn't like them. I know it sounds quite unbelievable but people do things like this all the time. Not only did I love them, they were exactly what I was looking for without the $2300 price tag.

As I write this, I look around at all the lovely things that surround me and remember the fun I had finding them, buying them and beautifying my home with them. The gaudy new reproductions don't even come close to the $3000 gold framed mirror that I bought years ago in Chicago for $100.

I have a unique small Asian chest with lots of little drawers, the kind an herbalist might have used and everyone who sees loves it and wants it. It's one of the few pieces that I cannot recall where it came from. I store rubber bands, paper clips, lamp finials, business cards, coins, pens and lots of other miscellaneous items in the small drawers and it beautifies my house while serving a purpose.

My coffee table and matching sofa table came from a consignment store and they are truly one of a kind elegant and so beautiful that I didn't hesitate to pay $1,500 for the pair. Lately I've started doing some research, because I think might be Maitland - Smith, which would be very exciting as they would be even more valuable than I first believed.

If you have never heard of Maitland-Smith, you should definitely check out the exquisite things this company puts out. Last year I found a Maitland-Smith chandelier at a local garage sale for $400. I was actually on my way to an estate sale I was doing, but I felt compelled to check out this sale. Good thing I did, because I sold that chandelier for $2,850! I didn't see a manufacturer label when I was buying it, but I knew it was very high-quality and absolutely beautiful even sitting in pieces in a box. It had metal elephants all around supporting a large "bowl" that would extend down from the ceiling about 4 feet. I took a gamble because it was unique and elegant but really got happy after I took it home and saw the Maitland-Smith logo.

I was in a rush, but still ended up spending $900 in about 15 minutes. I gave the man a deposit of $600, got a list of my purchases and a signed receipt and went back the next day and picked up all my treasures. He had other things in the house that he wanted to sell, and the items that hadn't sold during the garage sale could now go home with me for a song. This was not your ordinary garage sale and I usually don't spend that much, but this man really had exquisite things.

There is a comfortable leather chair in my office that a major retailer is currently still selling for $1900. It was brand new when I acquired it as part of a large purchase and ultimately may have cost $10...it was a spectacular estate filled with exquisite items.

In that same estate purchase there was a large oil painting that went to consignment in another state and sold for $15,000 of which $9000 was mine. I sold a stunning brand new dining room set for $3600 and sold other beautiful lamps and décor pieces and artwork and furniture. I paid $8500 for everything and even without the pieces I couldn't bear to part with, ultimately the return was over $40,000!

I have the most beautiful bedding that came from the home of a famous major league baseball player a couple of years ago. His mother is an acquaintance and when her daughter-in-law wanted to clear out some of their decorator's choices from a house they had yet to occupy, my friend ended up literally with an SUV full of bedding. Three bed sets with matching pillows. It was so overwhelming that she sold all of it to me for only $60 just to get it out of her car!

I didn't exactly know what I was buying but the price was too good to ask questions. It took a while to untangle bedspreads and dust ruffles and twenty-some pillows because they were similar colors and could be interchanged, but I finally ended up with three brand new and very expensive sets. I didn't even try to sell them, just gave two as gifts and kept one that I love. The way I see it, my entire bed set cost $20 and for another $40 I made two of my friends very happy, while I relieved another friend from the burden of not knowing what to do with these unwanted bulky items.

I have an armoire in my bedroom that hides a large flat-screen TV. It was part of a bulk sale and though it's huge and was quite new at the time I bought it, I only paid around $100 for it.

All my trees and outdoor plants came from sales along with their beautiful decorative pots.

A couple of years ago, I found a wonderful custom made cabinet at an estate sale. It was a great piece and I knew by the looks of it that it was expensive...with a light green finish and a beautiful green granite top. It was a give-away price at $350 but I had no place for it. I made an offer of $150 anyway because it was simply too good to pass up. Since it was the last day of the sale, the seller didn't want to get stuck with it, so she accepted my offer.

RECYCLED ELEGANCE

I called my best friend, thinking this would be a perfect addition to his charming little home by the beach. The next day we picked up the cabinet along with an almost-new flat-screen TV from another private party for $150. We put the cabinet in his living room, with the TV on top and it was perfect. Even better...after we were done, I presented my friend with the original receipt I fished out of one of the drawers when I bought the piece. Would you believe they paid $3,600? Anything custom-made is pricey, but this was even more so because of the granite top. The retail price of the TV was $400, which brings the total retail price of the 2 pieces to $4000. And my friend paid only $300 for both. Would you rather pay $4000 or $300?

Or would you prefer to buy furniture in a box, and spend the weekend trying to assemble the pieces made of cheap particle board, and treated with toxic chemicals? There is no substitute for quality. That's why you can still get $2000 for a 20 year old dresser from Maitland-Smith, but you're lucky to get $20 for a 2 year old dresser from Ikea!

Another friend furnished her new home from garage sales. That was her intention as she was looking not to make money, but to find wonderful things for herself. When we first met years ago, she shared with me that she had paid $10,000 for her high-end name brand bedroom set and I shared with her that about $8,000 of that money went right down the drain.

Like many people, she had never been exposed to the idea of non-retail shopping. For her it was a brand new world that opened up and continues to be fun and exciting. She has told me many times that with her priceless education from me, the same things I'm sharing here with you, she would never again consider walking into a retail store and spending $10,000 on furniture.

Now she knows that she could have bought the same quality and the same brand name from someone else, who already spent the $10,000. She could buy it for under $2000, and take herself to Italy for a month with the savings.

A couple of years ago, some acquaintances had to sell their huge house and move into something smaller. They had a lot of outrageously expensive furniture that would not fit in their new home. The move was taking place within a month and all the extra furniture had to go.

They had a gorgeous bedroom set that came with an exorbitant $28,000 price tag but there was simply no way to fit it into their new bedroom. I called my attorney who had just moved into a new house and would you believe he bought that entire bedroom set for $2,000? You read it correctly; a $28,000 bedroom set for $2,000!

This is not something that comes along every 200 years; truly it happens every day! On a daily basis people have to get rid of something and someone is going to get an awesome deal. If you are a player in this game, you can come out a huge winner.

Would you be willing to pay $1500 for a $36,000 Karges hand-crafted bedroom set? It was almost 20 years old, but as one of the finest names in furniture, it was hand-made and exquisite. I resold it for $6,500 and the lucky buyers still got a fantastic deal.

RECYCLED ELEGANCE

You will love finding exquisite things for your home and you'll love discovering for yourself that there is absolutely no reason to throw money away on ridiculously overpriced retail furniture. You don't want to be paying toxic prices for toxic furniture!

CHAPTER 10

CHRISTMAS EVERY DAY

Wouldn't it be wonderful to have Christmas every day? I am not referring to the stressed-out, frazzled, credit-card-draining crisis that many adults currently experience as Christmas. For many people the spirit of Christmas has become the spirit of "*can't wait until it's over*".

The Christmas of your childhood is what I'm referring to, where you couldn't wait to wake up and run downstairs in pajamas to open all those wonderful gifts. The atmosphere was charged with anticipation and excitement and there was magic in the air.

When you make your living looking for treasures, many of your days will feel like Christmas. My friends and my students have heard me repeatedly compare this business to opening Christmas presents; every appointment, every sale, holds so much potential.

You never know what you're going to find on the other side of the door. There are exciting opportunities everywhere and behind every door are wonderful surprises, waiting for you to loosen the ribbon and un-wrap the gift.

Before walking into the home where I bought the dolls I had no idea that I would be hitting the jackpot that day. You never know...that's what makes this business so much fun! Especially when you compare it to a job where you drive to the same place and do the same boring thing every day, for pretty much the same amount of money every week.

When I leave my house to go treasure hunting, I always feel positive anticipation. As you rack up some of your own success stories, you will have a positive track record and a kind of energetic *pull* that propels you out of bed. I would not be going to garage sales after all these years if I didn't still find them exciting and fun as well as very profitable. This is the anti-depressant of the century!

On one occasion when I had a store, someone pulled up in a truck and asked if I wanted some furniture. It turned out to be a truck full of very nice stuff and he was helping a friend dispose of it. I kept asking if he wanted to sell it, but no, he just wanted to give it to me. He turned out to be the owner of a local restaurant and after he had generously given me a truck full of great furniture, he followed that up by giving me $200 worth of gift certificates to his restaurant! Thanks Joe! That was a fun Christmas day...in August!

There is another significant reason I am speaking of Christmas in July. In these economic times wouldn't it make sense to literally buy your Christmas presents in July? It certainly would if you can buy them for pennies on the dollar!

Since the only economy we have any control over is our own, this makes financial sense anytime. I started doing this many years ago and it just gets better every year. In my twenties I was married into a large family and my Christmas list consistently had over 16 people on it. Buying retail for all of them would have cost a fortune, so I did what I always do; turned to the secondary market.

I started by buying something here and there that I thought would make a great gift. Eventually I was buying all of my gifts *non-retail*. In case you are inclined to dismiss this as being cheap or feeling some kind of embarrassment let me show you why this makes so much sense.

By October I was done with my Christmas shopping and each gift was beautifully wrapped and stored away, ready for December. I cannot tell you how many tens of thousands of dollars I saved through the years. Doing this is not only an economic life-saver but you're also reducing your holiday stress to almost zero. While most people are running around all stressed out spending way too much money on mass-produced junk with very little value, I have a tree decorating party at my house. We play Christmas music and sing carols and hang all the lovely ornaments on the tree. I always have great food and eggnog and champagne....a small group of good friends enjoying the festive feeling of the holiday season and having fun creating beautiful memories.

When it comes to opening presents, everyone loves and appreciates my gifts because they are unique and because I have all year to think about who gets what, it always turns out to be the right thing for the right person.

It's a fact that when you shop in retail stores, you are paying ridiculous mark-ups. Buying at a garage sale, you pay well below even the wholesale price. Someone else already paid the retail price and because they no longer want that item you can have it for pennies-on the-dollar. If you take nothing else out of this book, just this one mental shift will allow you to be a generous giver while holding on to a much bigger portion of your money. Wouldn't it be wonderful to give gifts that are unique and different, not just something you bought last minute because time was running out?

A couple of years ago I found a pair of brand new UGG boots in the original box at a garage sale. The $190 original price tag was still on the box, yet they sold it to me for $10! What a fabulous Christmas gift at an unbelievable price!

Although retailers would have us believe differently, there is absolutely nothing noble about throwing money away. They spend tens of millions of dollars brain-washing us to buy their products. One reason they have to charge so much, is because they have to keep up the expensive brain-washing process, called *advertising*. The irony here is that we pay for our own brain-washing.

The most prominent theme in this book is to encourage people to think outside the box and by doing so, hold on to more of their money. The sole purpose of retail advertising is to separate you from your money. Don't believe the lies...your responsibility is to yourself and your family...not to their corporate bottom line.

Also consider that in the course of traditional Christmas shopping you go to the same corporate-owned stores and have a selection from the same items that hundreds of thousands of other people are choosing from. This is limited and very boring. The idea of Christmas shopping at garage/moving sales has so many advantages. If you attend sales on most weekends during the summer, you will have been to dozens of them over the summer months and will have come across an incredible variety of items.

When I'm buying gifts at garage/estate/moving sales, there are two things that I look for, although it's not a hard and fast rule. I either want something that's clearly old (meaning vintage or antique, as opposed to *used*) or I am looking for something brand new, preferably still in its original box. A few weeks ago I found a brand new "Cranium" game for a dollar. I was not looking for anything like that but it's completely sealed and I could think of several people who would appreciate it. I looked it up and was surprised to see that particular edition selling for $69.98 in the retail world. Not bad for a dollar!

One of my friends recently showed me a beautiful bowl that she purchased as a Christmas gift for someone. It's brand new, still in the original box and she paid a total of $10 dollars for it at a garage sale. She has thanked me often for teaching her to shop this way and she thanked me again when an online search revealed her bowl currently selling for $135 at one of the finer department stores. Way to go! That's exactly how you do it!

People hold on to beautiful and expensive wedding gifts that they never use, and ultimately these end up in a garage sale. Something else you will find plenty of at these sales is brand new clothing that people never returned to the stores, or gifts that they didn't bother to exchange. When people have money, they simply don't want to deal with it, even if it's hundreds of dollars' worth of merchandise. Some are too shy or feel it's beneath them or they're too busy or most often, they just don't care. Whatever the reason, the expensive things with the price tags still attached end up selling in a garage sale for next to nothing.

Since you have read this far, hopefully, you have stopped asking why someone would sell a $135 item for $10. It goes back to what I've been saying throughout this book. When people want to get rid of something all they think about is how to accomplish that in the fastest and easiest way possible. They already made peace with the fact that they are not going to get a great deal of money for it and if they can get a few dollars it won't feel like a complete loss.

When it comes to garage sales, there is also the 'volume factor' to consider. They may be getting only a few dollars for each item, but when you add it all together, the money adds up.

It's interesting that if you were standing in someone's living room and offered them five dollars for a vase, they would probably be offended. However, garage sales are known for low prices, it's an unwritten expectation and they will be happy under those circumstances to sell it to you for just a couple of dollars. Don't try to figure it out. People will sell things for ridiculous prices, especially when they don't want to have to take it back inside.

Here is another great time-and-money saving tip I mentioned earlier: When I find something at a sale that's brand new, attractive and ridiculously well priced, I buy it and hold on to it. I have a cabinet where I keep all these goodies and if I need a gift for someone quickly, I am sure to find something in there. I have things like expensive ties and pen sets or pretty vases, beautiful costume jewelry, small, elegant picture frames, etc. all these are new and in their original box or new with tags.

I also have a large selection of cards for every occasion (also from garage sales, of course). If I'm invited to a birthday party, I don't have to stress out and run around looking for a card and a gift and wrapping paper and tissue paper and the little gift bag. I just go to my cabinet and I have everything.

People are selling fine stationery and expensive little gift bags all the time. When you see it, buy it. My gifts always get extra attention because they are beautiful and unique and have a definite "rich and expensive" feel to them even though I bought them for pennies on the dollar.

If you need Christmas related items, the best time to look for them is during the summer months. I have seen $200 dollar Christmas trees often in an unopened box selling for $10 or $20. Why would you wait and pay more? The stands for live trees usually sell for just a couple of dollars at garage sales during the summer. Why pay $50 at a department store in December?

I have the most exquisite ornaments and Christmas decorations, collected over the years from garage sales. Many of my ornaments sell for over a hundred dollars but the most I ever paid was $5. I certainly don't need any more, so I'm selective and I only buy them if they are unique and beautiful.

When you begin to see all that can be yours for next to nothing, you'll understand how it's easy to save thousands of dollars while acquiring things that are not only unique and exquisite but outstanding in quality and workmanship. I pay a lot of attention to quality and detail and have an issue with massed-produced cheap junk...especially when it's selling for ridiculous mark-up prices.

As you get more and more involved in this business, you will easily distinguish the fine quality items from the undesirable ones. If you are someone who already appreciates the finer things in life, you will be ecstatic with the top of the line treasures that can be yours for unbelievable prices.

CHAPTER 11

WHAT NOT TO DO

Avoid costly mistakes that could devour your profits.

Stay on track...

The treasures game is a little like playing poker. Just as you wouldn't start jumping up and down if you had a straight flush, you have to keep it cool and maintain a certain level of detachment in the midst of your deals. I once took a friend along for the ride on one of my appointments and was quite unpleasantly surprised when she started complimenting everything and expressing regret that the sellers had to part with such lovely things.

She was genuine and just being herself but this was not the reason I drove 20 miles to meet with complete strangers. I was on an appointment to buy things but she seemed to have completely gone unconscious and was on her own appointment; genuinely bothered because these people were selling some of their beautiful things. When the conversation took yet another unexpected turn, I finally had to step in and regain control. I caught up with her somewhere in the 50's and yanked her back to current time and the purpose of our visit. She was so caught up that I feared when we got to prices she might actually start bidding against me on behalf of the sellers and I would have to gag her and tie her up in the car so I could get some business done.

These people had beautiful things including an incredible partners' desk, and a Mont Blanc desk set and pens but they were selling the stuff because they were moving to a new house and probably wanted something new.

They were done with the stuff and ready to move, and now they were looking to me to pay something close to their asking price (remember I never quote prices first) and make their life easier by removing the stuff they didn't want. Ultimately, it's none of our business why people are selling and the lesson here is to maintain a friendly, but professional demeanor and stay on track as much as possible. If you take someone with you on an appointment be sure to put them under a gag-order.

Never, ever go anywhere even slightly dangerous...

If you don't feel comfortable don't go in! Seriously...this requires no further explanation!

After being in hundreds of homes, I am happy to say that I never had an unpleasant experience. These days it's easy to stay in touch with someone while in a strange house. In my earlier days, before cell phones, I sometimes said that my husband was a policeman and I was expecting him to meet me there any minute. This is not advice... just a bit of common sense.

Not doing the math...

WHAT NOT TO DO

I very rarely (never) buy things just to double my money. While 100% profit is nothing to sneeze at, that's not what I consider an exciting deal. Small items are not worth it and large items require a bigger financial risk...the bigger the price, the bigger the risk. I would not be excited to spend $400 on something that would only potentially resell for $800 unless it was an immediate and sure turn around. If you are not buying things for yourself; it's all about the profit margin and if the profit potential doesn't thrill you, wait for one that does.

One of my friends bought a huge amount of car mats once, thinking she would make some great money reselling them. The mats were very nice and she got an excellent price of $5 per set and could resell easily for $10. Had she asked for my advice prior to jumping into that silly deal I would certainly have talked her out of it.

Here's why: Unless you have a distribution channel for all those mats you will go crazy trying to sell them one at a time. If she goes to the swap meet (which was her plan) and sells 20 sets a day, she will only make $200 dollars. Let's not forget that 20 mats cost her $100, so after paying for the space and spending her time, we're talking about *losing* money. Aside from the fact that selling 20 sets is an optimistic goal, because car mats are not very high on anyone's desire list. Buying those mats would only have made sense, if she took samples to auto-related places and pre sold them in volume, with an up-front deposit.

Before you jump into what sounds like a great deal, play it out in your mind. Also make sure that you are willing to do all that it takes to create the results that you are envisioning.

Know your limitations...

You have to know yourself and what you will and won't do. For example, I know that I would not be happy spending my weekends doing swap meets. Since I have this attitude, it would be foolish to go against my nature and pursue something swap-meet related just for the money. It's difficult to create success with something you hate doing.

I know many people who make a very successful living from weekend swap meets. I'm thinking of two acquaintances in particular who have become wealthy. Their wives have never worked outside the house, they both have lovely homes, their kids all went to college and they have a very good lifestyle... all from buying things during the week and reselling at the swap meet on Saturdays and Sundays. One of them has done this quietly and successfully for over 35 years. How fun to do what you enjoy and never have say the words "*my boss*".

My friend with the car mats loves hanging out and schmoozing with everyone who walks by. This is a fun day for her.....if only she had remembered to pencil out the financial details before buying all those mat sets.

Spending good time on bad things...

One of our most important and most valuable commodities is our time. Don't allow yourself to get caught up with inexpensive items that can chew up your precious time. I once bought a bottle of nail polish for a quarter and I liked the color so much that I bought it in spite of the fact that it had spilled at some point and now there was dried, caked up polish all over the top of the bottle.

When I got home, I spent time using pliers to get it open and my energy and polish-remover cleaning it up until I realized how much time I was wasting and tossed it in the trash. My little voice had told me not to get it even if they gave me money to go with it, but I ignored it so I spent time on something so very trivial.

If you get bogged down in meaningless activities, you run the risk of using up your energy without producing any measurable results and it will make you ineffective and hurt your profits in the long run. So...don't piddle!

Painting, cleaning, fixing, re-upholstering...

I stay far away from things that need repair and one of the costliest repairs is upholstery. If you could buy a chair for $2 knowing that you could sell it for $200 after getting it re-upholstered, would you buy it? I sure wouldn't. An average price for recovering an average chair is around $150. Even if you already have the fabric and you would save that expense, your price is no longer $2 for the chair, now its $152. After you invest your time in taking it to the upholsterer and picking it up, you are losing money!

Even if the upholsterer is next door, we are not in the business of spending $150 to make a $50 profit. Same principle applies to having something restored, repaired, etc. Anytime you have to pay someone to make your item sellable, you are giving up a big chuck of money for no good reason. The running around, follow up time, the money and the energy.......you could be using all that to buy something else and turn it over quickly.

Vacillating on a good deal...

As I've been saying throughout the book, when you find something that is one of those 'too good to be true' deals, pay for it immediately and put it in your car. If you pay immediately the seller is not likely to change his mind but if it's in your car it's an irrevocably done-deal. Sometimes people get emotional and unreasonable and the best way to avoid hassles is to secure your purchase and get it out of their sight.

Never point out how dumb they were for selling something so cheap...

One would think this is a no-brainer, but I've seen it happen too many times. I'm always dumbfounded that someone would think it's a good idea to go back and gloat about the profit they made to the same person from whom they bought the thing for almost nothing.

One of my girlfriends has a very annoying acquaintance, who showed up during a sale a group of us were having in a clubhouse. He bought a piece of furniture from one of the girls for $25 and leaving it right where it was, he camped out at our sale until he resold it for $300! This is so disturbing on so many levels...and he wonders why nobody likes him. I didn't know this was going on until after the fact, but you can be sure he will never be allowed at any of our sales again. Our objective is to have win-win situations and when you leave you want people to thank you as you thank them in return.

WHAT NOT TO DO

Drive-by garage sale shopping...

I often see people (not handicapped in any way) pull up in their car, often on the wrong side of the street and check out the entire sale from the curb. This is absolutely unacceptable for someone who is creating a business. People who are too lazy to get out of their cars are not going to get any good deals. Sometimes they even lower their window and yell out asking for prices! They only crawl out of the car after wasting time, interrupting and annoying others by shouting out questions. In response to these drive-by slugs, I made a sign once with large letters that said "*Please get out of the car*". It got a lot of laughs, but seriously....how lazy can you be?

Allowing the seller to determine how much you will spend...

When you are considering a purchase, you must have an idea of how much you're willing to pay. It doesn't matter what the seller wants. If there is not a substantial profit in it for you, you are not interested. I gave a formula earlier, so that you have some guidelines and feel safe. It's completely unnecessary to take risks with your money. There is an endless supply of incredible deals out there, so don't disqualify yourself from future opportunities by spending foolishly. Stick to the *no-brainer* deals.

Becoming emotionally involved...

Do not become emotionally attached to anything you buy or attached to getting your way. This is not a battle of wills and you are also not here to gamble. Something that's a good deal at one price becomes a bad deal at another price. Unless you are shopping for yourself, there are not many things on the list of must-haves. If the item is so awesome that you know you can turn it over for a great profit, just buy it. Pay the best negotiated fair price and get on with it.

If you have things you wish to sell, your first order of business would be to establish a value. By the time a buyer comes along, you as the seller must know what you have and how much you want for it. You also want to know in advance the lowest price that you will accept.

Appraiser not the buyer...

It's the seller's job to determine a price and a value. Never ask a dealer who is there to buy something to appraise it for you....it's an obvious conflict of interest.

It's rather absurd to ask a dealer to reveal the value of something he's about to buy for pennies on the dollar. If I tell you a ring is worth $500 but I only want to pay $50, you won't sell it to me. If I tell you it's worth $50 you won't believe me because I'm a dealer and you know I'm going to resell it for a profit.

People often ask me values on things I'm interested in buying, and I always have to tell them politely that I'm not the right person to ask. This is simple laziness on the part of the seller and the free appraisal could cost him a bundle. I can only tell someone what I'm willing to pay. It's the simple truth and people will respect you for telling it.

Hoarding the stuff...

WHAT NOT TO DO

When first starting out you might be tempted to hold on to all these newly acquired goodies that were such a bargain. Don't do it...you are in the business of buying and selling not buying and hoarding. If you don't re-sell you dry up the money flow, and you will also end up completely overwhelmed. If you get to a point where you have too much, you have to stop buying and work diligently on selling.

I know from personal experience when people get overwhelmed with too much stuff, they just want to get rid of it and you could end up losing money instead of making a profit. This is the main reason we find such good deals in the first place. People have too much or too much to do and getting rid of it and getting their sanity back is more important to them than the money. I still have to be careful about falling into this trap.

The exceptions to this are jewelry, coins, diamonds, and other small valuables. Anything in precious metals will continue to go up and if you don't need the money right now, it's a good idea to hold on to them. I purchased 2 Franklin Mint sterling silver sets of bank ingots some years ago for $150 each. When sterling went up I sold them for $1,500 each. I didn't check the values when I bought them; I just knew they were worth much more than what I paid. I like to surprise myself by waiting to find out values until I'm actually thinking of selling something. A $300 investment turning into $3000 is always exciting!

I also bought miscellaneous sets and pieces of sterling silver and saved them for a while. I may have paid two or three hundred dollars total and sold the entire bunch for $4,300. Not bad!

I bought a diamond ring once for $150 and held on to it for a few years. When I finally decided to sell it, I got an unbelievable $7,000 for it! As long as I was not looking to sell it, I didn't have it checked out, and was quite surprised that it was so valuable. Another time I took a bunch of broken gold that I had saved for several years and sold it to a dealer for $3,400.

You can't go wrong with gold and silver. This is my personal opinion and not investment advice, but I have yet to meet someone who regretted holding on to gold and silver. I have however met many people who held on to many other things and got themselves into a state of paralysis by doing so.

Taking the first offer...

If you have something that you think might be valuable, you should have at least three dealers look at it. This is part of the process of establishing a resale value.

I tell potential buyers honestly that I will be getting three bids, but I never reveal what offers I've received unless I am using that information as a bargaining chip. No matter how good it sounds, never, ever, allow someone to pressure you into taking the first offer. If their offer is legitimate, it will still be there a few days later. Also, find your own dealers. Never ask a dealer to recommend another dealer....it could be his cousin.

Selling things without checking out their value...

WHAT NOT TO DO

This applies to everything, especially jewelry. You must get a jeweler's magnifying glass and look over each piece carefully...and I mean carefully. Look for markings and look for names in vintage pieces. Buy a diamond tester and a gold tester and make sure you know what you have. A diamond tester won't tell you the value, but it will tell you if it's a diamond and after that you can go to different jewelers and ask what they would pay for it and if it's a large stone you may want to get a certified appraisal.

When it comes to furniture, the better companies always put their name on their items. For a dresser, a desk or nightstand, look in the top drawers. The company name is usually branded into the left side panel inside the drawer. Always check, because there is a huge difference in names and prices.

The better furniture pieces will be apparent in the quality of the workmanship. An important feature of good quality furniture is dove-tailed drawers. Make sure to check for this. If it's not wood and the drawers are just glued in, and there is no name, it's not a serious piece of furniture. You can still buy it, if it's a give-away price, and then…..give it away.

Not securing your purchase…

For some odd reason I'm not a big stickler for receipts. I suppose this would be the professional thing to do, but I never really got in the habit of doing it. If I buy something that I have to pick up later, I trust that it will be there without any hassles when I go back and interestingly enough, it always has been. I pay for things up front or leave a deposit and I have only had two experiences in all my years where people didn't honor the deal.

There is something however that I am a stickler over; I always take something with me. If it's a sofa, I take a cushion, a dresser, I take a drawer. I take the remote from the TV or a shelf from a bookcase. If you take something it makes the item un-sellable and removes temptation. I have been lucky and have dealt with wonderful and honest sellers, but sometimes it's beyond their control. The kids or spouses could get involved because they want more money or a neighbor could come over and mess up your deal. When the drawer is missing no such problem arises.

I am very adamant about doing this and highly recommend that you make it a must-do, as well. I never tell the seller the reason. If you paid for it, it's yours and can take with you whatever you want but there's no need to insult or offend. You could be taking it to see how it matches your décor, to show your spouse, to buy matching fabric, to take some of the weight; to prevent something from getting lost, etc. your reason is your secret. I find this to be more valuable than a receipt.

I bought an antique chaise in Palos Verdes, California once, and I neglected to follow my own advice. The next morning the seller's daughter (who previously showed zero interest) came over and decided to take *my* chaise to an auction in L.A.

There was no arguing with this guy; in fact he was upset because I was not being understanding. They were wealthy and didn't need to drag furniture to auction but it was my fault, for not practicing what I preach. Even if you have a bill of sale, it's not worth the ugly fight if someone refuses to honor their part.

However, if you have the cushion, they don't have much choice.

Buying junk...

The fact that you can buy lots of things for only a few dollars doesn't mean you should. If you don't see yourself using it and it doesn't have any resale value, walk away. Even if you get something free, it's not an asset if it clutters up your life. The stuff accumulates quickly and you will end up treading water, trying to get out from under it all. When you buy one or two items of quality and distinction, you may pay a bit more, but it feels good and you can move forward in re-selling them. If you spend that same amount on twelve things that are not quality, you will have a sense of clutter and an urgency to get rid of it. Walk away, and save your money for the next sale.

Handling the merchandise...

If someone offered you $50,000 for your grand piano and all you had to do was deliver it to the buyer, you would not call your cousin Fred to throw it on the back of his pick-up truck. Indeed, you would be extremely careful to get it there without a scratch so you can collect your money.

Everything you buy represents a certain dollar amount. You have to learn how to handle fine furniture and valuables. You also have to learn not to scratch up walls and scrape the bottoms of paintings by dragging them on the floor.

All breakables have to be carefully wrapped and jewelry and silver has to be protected against being tossed about and getting scratched or the stones getting beat up.

Never, ever stand things up in the back of the car because they will fall over the second you step on the gas. Even tall boxes can flip over suddenly, if not wedged. Think three steps ahead to avoid disasters. Handling valuable merchandise is 25% art and a love for beautiful things and 75% common sense. If you sell online and have to ship things, be sure to pack in anticipation of the box being thrown about like that old luggage commercial on TV where gorillas toss a suitcase repeatedly around the cage and jump up and down on it. The suitcase made it fine...the contents of your package will have to survive also.

The condition of the merchandise is reflected in the condition of the home...

Sloppy people who live in a mess are probably going to have things that are also in sloppy condition. If they neglect their living space, their personal belongings will most likely reflect that same lack of caring. These are the individuals that have clothing with stains that can only be removed with scissors; they have broken appliances, dirty furniture and almost everything they own needs repair. It's like a plague has spread through all their belongings and even healthy things die faster than they would in a different environment.

You have to use extra caution. I was at a house once and the grass and weeds in the back yard looked like they hadn't been cut in 25 years. I was just about to step off the patio when my uncle grabbed my arm in mock-horror and said "Unless you're looking for an elephant, don't go in that jungle" He was right.... where was I going?

The home where I found the air cleaner in the garage was full of beautiful things in pristine condition, so it wasn't a great gamble to spend a few dollars and expect that it would work.

It's not necessary to take notes and be hyper-vigilant about these things. In no time at all you'll find your own rhythm and it really becomes second nature. As you get comfortable in this business you'll find things coming to you without great effort. Applying these common sense ideas could save lots of headaches... not to mention lots of cash. We want to have fun, enjoy the moments and make money without the struggle that many people believe they have to endure on a daily basis.

I found the following words recently in an ad from someone in network marketing. I think it captures the way many of us live...

Is your life like mine once was....being rudely awoken by an annoying alarm clock each morning....only to get dressed in the clothes that I had to buy for work...driving through morning traffic in a car that I was still paying for...in order to get to a job I needed...so I could pay for the clothes...pay for the car...and pay for the home that I left empty all day in order to afford to live in it...

Sometimes from the perspective of the treadmill we're on, we don't see the options that are available to us. I sincerely hope that in this book I've offered an option, a way to stop spending high dollar amounts on low value items, while creating an income stream that could make you seriously rich.

CHAPTER 12

FOCUS AND DISCIPLINE EQUALS WEALTH

Without a doubt, the valuable tips and ideas in this book can change your life in a big way. However, it will not help someone who is unwilling to do what it takes to improve their life. The one comment I hear consistently from people about my business is that I must have *an eye* or some special talent that they simply don't have.

I must admit, I do have one thing that's different. I've always had a burning desire **not** to have a 9-5 job. This business grew out of my need to have freedom in my life and to avoid working for somebody else. The rest was learn-as-you-go, self-taught, trial and error applications.

My other passion is beautiful and unique things. When I started in this business, as a teenager it was the beautiful things I fell in love with, but it was the incredible, stunning low prices that bedazzled my senses and put the unattainable at my fingertips that got me hooked for life. This world of exquisite things for pennies on the dollar allowed me to develop a flair for elegance and quality. The opportunities to cultivate a sense of style I attribute to the fact that I could buy names like Chanel, Gucci, Givenchy, Dior, Baccarat, Lalique and Bulgari etc., for below Sears-discount prices.

FOCUS AND DISCIPLINE EQUALS WEALTH

When it comes to high-end designer labels, the quality is undoubtedly far superior and there is a legitimate reason for higher prices but beyond that, buying famous designer name luxury items is a game, a cloak of mystery and un-attainability that the wealthy like to wrap around themselves.

It's merely a perception of value and the entire *designer* world carries a mystique, an implication of class, of sophistication and great style, chic elegance….it's not reality, it's simply an unspoken agreement to maintain a high desirability factor for an item because there's an exchange of something even more valuable to attain it…large amounts of money!

I realized a long time ago that while I adore the finer things in life, it's somewhat insane to let go of large sums of money to acquire any of it. Once you discover for yourself that for the same price you pay for disposable junk, you can buy something of outstanding quality because someone else already paid the retail price for it, you get hooked…it's really a lot of fun!

If you are not yet familiar, start today and get acquainted with the good stuff. Make it a point to pick up an expensive piece of porcelain or crystal, or a designer pair of shoes or handbag, or check out a high-end piece of furniture and compare it with some piece of junk at Wal-Mart. You will immediately see the difference because the quality, the material and the workmanship is unmistakably superior to some item mass produced in China. It's really quite obvious. Now you can consistently go for the finer things in life, while choosing wisely how much you will pay.

We are living in turbulent economic times to say the least and many people have gone from the good life to survival-mode almost overnight. But, life can turn on a dime...any minute of any day. I'm showing you a way to have the most exquisite things you can imagine, for just pennies on the dollar as well as make a lot of money in the process. All you have to do is to get started and stay with it, apply the information in this book and stay focused, focused, focused. My exciting deals came to me because I stayed on track and went on all the appointments and consistently read the classified ads and I was willing to get in the car and go check something out, even if the weather was bad, even if I was tired, even if I had a headache.

It was raining the day I bought the dolls. I had dinner plans with friends that evening, but I gave the seller a deposit for the dolls and told him I would be back shortly. I didn't know how valuable they were, but I had trained myself to complete my deals as quickly as possible. I could have called and said I will come by in the morning, but my sense of discipline insisted that I go back immediately with the rest of the payment and take my purchase home.

As I said before, the longer you leave things and the more time people have to sleep on it, the higher the risk that something will happen to undo your deal. On my way to pick up the dolls, I stopped by the restaurant where my friends were waiting and kidnapped my girlfriend's brother to help me. We loaded up the car in the rain and unloaded the dolls at my house. After that, we all had a nice dinner and a great time. By handling your affairs and honoring your word you truly increase your chances of success dramatically.

FOCUS AND DISCIPLINE EQUALS WEALTH

I was going through some personal papers recently and came across the following words. DISCIPLINE EQUALS FREEDOM. I don't remember when I wrote it, nor where it came from, but I have a habit of writing down thoughts that strike me as valuable and I believe those words have profound wisdom and truth.

Discipline can make the difference between success and failure. It's imperative to instill in yourself the '**do it now'** mentality and not allow thoughts or activities to distract you from your success. I don't know any successful people who approach their business with negligence and sloppiness and not suffer the consequences. Conversely, you reap the rewards of being on top of things, by spending the extra time to do things right.

As the old saying goes "If you don't have the time to do it right the first time, how will you find the time to do it over?" This one also applies to your energy; if you're too tired to deal with it now when it just takes a few minutes, you will surely be too tired to deal with it later, when it's a full blown disaster.

Neglect can turn an $85 dollar traffic ticket into a warrant for your arrest and cause much anxiety and unnecessary expense. You have to know that you can count on yourself, because truly you are the one and only person responsible for your life.

It may be easier to turn on the TV instead of dealing with whatever requires our attention, but neglect is a disease and it can destroy lives. It's slow and insidious and one of the most destructive habits we can allow. I say allow because it's a choice and people who allow the emotion that says *"I don't feel like it"* to run their life deprive themselves of a great life by indulging their temporary emotions.

A friend puts it this way regarding his diligence toward exercise; *"The pain of regret far outweighs the pain of discipline"*. Doesn't that make so much sense? It's like dieting....if you don't handle it when it's a 20 pound problem, how will you handle it when it's an 80 pound problem??

What does this have to do with this business? Everything! It has everything to do with your success. This applies to every area of life and because I want you to succeed, I am giving you the best of everything that will contribute to your success.

This is so huge that if you apply just this chapter to your life, it will have been worth hundreds of times the price of this book. Everything begins with our thoughts.

Did you know that 93% of people who buy opportunity books never even open them?? Our comfort zone is so compelling that the majority of individuals go right back to doing what they were doing even if it means being depressed and miserable.

There are tons of self-help books on the market and they cover everything from anxiety to procrastination and everything in between. You can go out and buy all the books to figure out why your habits are not conducive to success, but reading a book or having the insight as to the why of it, most likely will not solve the problem.

Our issues are buried in the subconscious and cannot be solved by the intellect. Most of our thoughts and habits originated in our childhood, not the events that happened to us, but the meaning we gave to those events. That's another book entirely, a very fascinating subject, but for now you must get clear and get real with yourself that only you can change your habits.

The words of "discipline equals freedom" might also be expressed as DISCIPLINE EQUALS WEALTH. There are many paths to becoming wealthy. I am only giving you one of them here. This wonderful business is faster, more exciting and a lot more fun than most others, but you will still have to show up and do what is required of you.

The secret code is still *focus and discipline*. If you get into the groove and keep your mind focused, you will literally attract deals and more deals to come to you. When I started my days by reading the classifieds and happily working my business, all sorts of unbelievable deals came my way. When I spent the week distracted with other things, and just went to garage sales on Saturdays, I still did well but attention and looking for deals consistently really produced incredible results.

This is one of the greatest secrets of life: **energy flows where attention goes**. Whatever you put your attention (thoughts) on; the subconscious mind magnifies and brings you more. This is not just some new age philosophy; you can test it out and know it for yourself. When you get into the flow of things, you will be amazed at what shows up practically on your doorstep.

One day I was inspired by the idea of a new car, meaning *new to me,* <u>not</u> new from the dealer. I had a long list in my head of everything that I wanted this car to have. I kept mentally refining that list, without knowing what make or model I wanted, just thinking of what it would feel like to experience all those qualities in my new car. I didn't even know if there was a car out there that had all these things I was contemplating. I simply had a strong feel for what I wanted.

I was living in Chicago at the time and the first priority on my list was that my car had to be higher off the ground than other cars because the snow in the winter was a big problem. I also wanted a four-wheel drive, though I wasn't exactly sure what that was, just that it wouldn't get stuck in the snow. This was in the 80's and SUV's were not around yet, or if they were, I knew nothing of them.

I wanted a rich, leather interior and wanted it to be luxurious on the inside. And I was super attracted to the idea of a car phone, which was something most people didn't even contemplate at that time.

I also love music and play it all the time while driving, so a fabulous stereo system was a must. Low miles and perfect condition were also important and because of the nature of my business I absolutely had to have lots of cargo room. And of course, what's always on my list was that this wonderful car had to have a fabulous price.

This story is so good, because it's truly a testament to how the Universe unfolds when you allow yourself to think only about what you want and don't worry about how it's going to show up. You just have to trust that it will be there. I placed an ad in the

FOCUS AND DISCIPLINE EQUALS WEALTH

classifieds to sell my old car and much to my surprise it sold the day the ad came out.

Wow! I had not counted on such fast results! I hadn't even started looking for my dream car and now here I was with no car at all. No problem, you just have to keep the faith that the perfect thing is right around the corner. My next move was to get out the classified ads and start looking.

This is where the story gets a little weird, but oh so cool. In this case the perfect thing was not around the corner, it was...**across the street**!!

I found the perfect car, one of those gems that stay with you in memory as something you truly loved having in your life. It was an AMC Eagle, something I had never even heard of. Not only was it a 4-wheel drive, but it was also a station wagon with lots of cargo room and amazingly enough, it was higher off the ground than other cars. And just like I had dreamed, it was all leather interior, a great stereo, and if all that doesn't blow you away....it had a car phone!

The car belonged to the owner of a printing company. In fact I was acquainted with him because I once lived in that building. He hardly ever drove the car, just had it around for rush-deliveries, and such. He had a phone installed for himself and upgraded the stereo system. The car was show-room condition with very low miles on it.

It was getting very little use and taking up his parking space, so he wanted to get rid of it. The price was ridiculously low and all I had to do to buy it was walk directly across the street!

You will see wonderful, mysterious things happen regularly as you start to focus your attention on what you want. This car had every single feature that I had envisioned in my mind….right down to the car phone! Seriously…what are the chances!?

The only thing I didn't love about the car was the only thing I never even considered….the color. It was two-toned, yellow and brown and besides not being very attractive, everyone knew where I was by my car. The inside however was very luxurious and I never got stuck in the snow. It was truly a spectacular car and way ahead of its time and I loved it and even more I love the story of how it came to me.

I got such a sweet deal on my Eagle that I was able to make one of my other dreams come true…..a white four door Jaguar. I was crazy about those cars and just like I said before, when you believe that you can have it and don't worry about the "how", it will find its way into your life.

This was the perfect scenario, now I had my work car and I had my dream car. The Jaguar rarely left the garage in the winter and I had my other perfect car to haul things around in without scratching up the white beauty.

I got an extraordinary deal on the Jaguar too, but I have to admit that I had trouble with it immediately. A few days after I bought it, I put on my tightest jeans and did my hair and makeup, thinking that we (me and my new car) needed to get our picture taken.

I asked my step-dad, to do the honors, by going with me down to Lake Michigan where he could take some very lovely pictures of me draped across the hood of my fabulous new car that would surely be the envy of all my friends.

Unfortunately, it was just not my day. The minute we got to the lake my beautiful, sleek white Jaguar mysteriously died and had no interest whatsoever in coming to life again.

Much to my distress and my stepfather's amusement, we finally had to call a tow-truck and even worse, had to call my mom to pick us up, though I would have preferred instead to walk the 58 blocks home. To complete my day from hell, my step-dad was not about to let the photo-op go to waste. Unfortunately, the pictures were not of me sitting on the hood like the models at the car shows with the wind blowing through my hair.

It cost a few dollars to get the Jaguar to be all that it could be, but after that we got along perfectly and I had many wonderful memories and plenty of the pictures I had envisioned.

My mom and dad and my uncle kept themselves entertained with my story and the tow-truck pictures and got lots of good laughs out of it. When it comes to keeping you humble, you can count on your family!

Even with the additional money spent on repairs, I came out slightly on top when I sold the car a few years later. You may not be able to negotiate the price of bread and milk and utilities, but the luxuries should not take a financial toll on your bank account. That's why you want to buy things only when they are radically below market price. That way, regardless of what happens there is enough of a profit margin that you won't lose your shirt.

As a side note here, one might ask, didn't I have someone look at the car before buying it, and the answer is no. I bought and sold quite a few cars and I had to make a quick assessment most times. The deals were so good that by the time I could get my mechanic, the car would have sold 10 times. A Jaguar was a luxury, and more of a liability than an asset as they were notorious for having problems and being expensive to repair. But it was *something I had to have* and figured the super-good price gave me some cushioning for repairs, should they be needed.

The reason we go to work...once our necessities are handled, is to have the things and the life-style that brings us pleasure. I think it's a sad misconception that we have to *do without*. If you are attracted to something and it feels good to contemplate having it in your life....you should have it.

I always had a great passion and love for this business and I share this story because the amazing things that at the time I thought were just falling into my lap, I can see now in retrospect, came to me because I was focused and disciplined. In my earlier years I was not quite so organized and certainly not very disciplined. It's something that I had to work on, mostly because I didn't know how to stop fighting myself and make it easy.

I can tell you that discipline is one of the greatest habits you can master and it will pay off in rewards for the rest of your life. It's one of the key components of self-esteem because you know you are on top of things and not just tossed about by random circumstances life throws your way. It feels good to know that you can trust yourself to take care of YOU.

Being organized is a large part of discipline and I cannot stress enough the value of cultivating these traits until they become your habitual ways of being. Your success is greatly hindered, your stress level goes up and your self-esteem goes down when you are disorganized. Sloppy efforts get sloppy and sporadic results.

The first and most important area of life to begin applying discipline is where life happens first...our **thinking**. Most people don't realize that thoughts are a creative force. Most of the fifty-some thousand thoughts we have each day, are the same as yesterday, which are the same as all the previous yesterdays. The same things keep showing up because we keep thinking the same thoughts!

When we get more of what we don't want, we give our attention to it, by complaining about it and being upset about it and asking the *why me* questions about it and worrying even more about it and...we continue to attract more of what we don't want.

That's why the rich get richer and the poor get poorer. It's not because the poor are the unfortunate ones who have to do without, so the rich can have all the money and all the good stuff! It's because the poor think thoughts of lack and limitation and they worry (obsessive thinking) about the bills they can't pay and the rent they can barely scrape together.

They worry about the car breaking down or the kids needing braces. It's the thoughts of *not-enough* that sends out a vibration and *not-enough* is what keeps showing up.

Too many people put their energy into finding a job with good benefits and then keeping that job even if it makes them miserable. Eight hours of their day goes into working on someone else's business and someone else's dream, so they can keep a job they hate. That's why every Monday morning roughly a million Americans call in sick. Wow!

According to some surveys 87% of our population dislikes their job. That ends up costing about $150 billion per year in treatment for stress-related problems, absenteeism, reduced productivity and employee turnover.

It's draining and discouraging to spend our days in an environment that makes us unhappy. When the paycheck comes, the problem is compounded by the fact that it's simply not enough. People feel bad about not having money to go on vacation; they feel bad about not having money to send their kids to better schools. They think about all the wonderful things in life they can't have and feel left out and angry because they can't afford them.

Conversely...the rich think about money and how to make more of it. They think about deals. They think about the luxuries of life they already enjoy and which exotic location would be best for Christmas, or if there is room next week at the Ritz in Paris.

Wealthy individuals don't shop with the price tag as a consideration. They don't agonize over how much things cost and how to manipulate their credit cards to buy something they can't afford. They have a

FOCUS AND DISCIPLINE EQUALS WEALTH

wealth consciousness and the poor have a poverty consciousness.

It really is that simple. The Law of Attraction is no more personal than the Law of Gravity. The wealthiest and the poorest person on the planet will have the same result with the Law of Gravity when falling off a ten-story building. The gods don't play favorites by letting the poor guy hit the ground while sending angels to sweep up the rich guy and gently deposit him on a stack of velvet pillows.

There is no investment you can make that's more valuable than your own personal development. It's hardly possible to make changes in your life if you keep thinking the same thoughts that created the results you currently have.

In his book *"As a Man Thinketh"* written in 1903, James Allen, one of the great minds upon whose words the entire personal development industry was founded, offers us these profound words of wisdom:

"Right thinking begins with the words we say to ourselves. We are the architects of our own lives and unwittingly create pain and suffering for ourselves due to the unconscious thoughts we focus on within.

Every thought you think creates that very reality for you. If you see yourself as lacking and poor then you will be lacking and poor. If your thinking is going after and gaining wealth then wealth is what you will obtain. It's simple to manifest in your life whatever you desire.

What you think and do draws more of the same to you. Change your attitude and behavior to what you want drawn into your life."

Success continues to come to millions of people who use this profound life secret. Growing up in a communist country where "*not enough*" was everyone's experience and wealth was a non-existent dream; I had plenty of things to unlearn and un-program from my consciousness when I came to realize that the way the world is *sold* to us is not the truth at all.

My message throughout this book is to think outside the box. This business will offer you a new way of thinking, a new way to create extraordinary income, a new way to own fabulous beautiful things, a new way to decorate, a new way to live and enjoy the lifestyle and peace of mind that you deserve. I found my dreams hidden among the treasures...hopefully you will too.

THE END...or...THE BEGINNING?

www.ingramcontent.com/pod-product-compliance
Lightning Source LLC
Chambersburg PA
CBHW070234190526
45169CB00001B/186